Disclaimer

This book is designed purely for information purposes, for enjoyment for your dogs and in no way is a substitute for veterinary advice. You should always consult your vet prior to commencing a new diet for your beloved pets and also check out the possibility of any underlying illnesses, usually fulfilled by a veterinary check-up and blood tests.

The author of this book takes no responsibility for errors or omissions, changes or alterations in the current dog world, nor any consequential events regarding any of the recipes or descriptions held in the text.

Acknowledgements

Table of Contents

Disclaimer 1
Acknowledgements 2
Table of Contents 3
INTRODUCTION 6
What are the Pros and Cons of Vegan/Vegetarian Diets? 10
The Best Dog Bowl Ever! 13
Supplements for Dogs 20
Making Your Own Calcium Supplement 30
Power for Puppies! 32
Doggie Hygiene – Homemade Soaps/Conditioners to Smell Nice! 35
    Basic Soap Recipe   36
Massage Therapy for Dogs 39
Care in Making Homemade Doggie Dishes 42
    Classic Kibble Recipe   44
Make Your Own Dog Toys and Accessories – Hours of Fun! (?) 46
Our Recipes 50
Vegan 51
    How To Make Flax or Chia Eggs   52
    Honey and Sweet Potato Cookies   53
    Apple Bobbers   56
    Buster's Best Meatballs   58
    'Man Come – Mango' Fruit Leathers!   60
    Banana, Carrot and Oatie Bones   63
    Delicious Doggie Donuts   65

Charlie's Chocolate Drops	68
Furry Friends Falafels	70
Carrot, Date, and Oatmeal Treats	71
Blueberry Hummus	73
Cold Nose, Warm Heart Popsicles	75
Pups 'Popcorn'	77
Winter Warmer Vegan Stew	79
Sweet Potato, Almond and Lentil Surprise	81
Pear and Oat Doggie Biscuits	83
Rice and Buckwheat Goodie Tray	85
Quinoa and Almond Butter Yummies	87
Tofu and Vegetable Medley	89
No-Meat Doggie Meatloaf	91
Peanut Butter and Orange Cake	93
Leafy Lentil Loaf	95
Butternut Squash Muffins	97
Butternut Squash and Oat Cookies	99
Carrot and Parsley Cookies	101
Sweet Potato and Apple Surprises	103
Roasted Vegetables with Applesauce	105
Pumpkin Cookies	107
Sweet Potato and Parsnip Chews	109
Carrot Pate	111
Doggie Kale Chips	113

Lacto Vegetarian Dogs 114

Blueberry Cobbler	115
'Sausage and Mash' – Share this with Your Dogs!!	117
Cheesy Feet Bikkies	119
Doggata Frittata (Kale)	121
All Day Breakfast Veggie Style	123
Snowman Frozen Fruit Treats	125
Pooch Pizzas	127

Lacto Ovo Vegetarian 130
    Eggy Macaroni Cheese Bake   131
    Porridge   133
    Kedgie-Veggie   135
    Doggie Scotch Eggs   137
    Luxury Lacto Lasagne   139
    Egg and Sweet Potato Rice   141
    Broccoli Mimosa   143

Pescetarian 145
    Cod, Pea and Mint Bites   146
    Sardine and Tomato Triangles   147
    Mackerel Scramble   149
    Salmon and Veggie Patties   151
    Tonno e Fagioli   153

Simple Home Remedies for Precious Pup/Daily Dog Problems 155

Other Homemade Remedies 161
    Nose Butter   162
    Dry and Cracked Paws Balm   163

INTRODUCTION

Vegetarian or Vegan – to feed or not to feed?

The way you feed your dog, is, of course, entirely your choice. It may be that you have environmental issues from which you discern your choices, or that your lifestyle of a vegetarian or vegan diet, or the relevant offshoots, determine the way you wish you and your pet to live, or simply (but not the best scenario), is that it can be easier to feed you and your family (including Henry Hound) on the same foods.

One thing is definite, so let us start by busting the myths. You love your dog/s, you want to do the best for them and in return they give that love back a million-fold. Dogs are OMNIVORES, not carnivores, as many misguided people would like us to believe. Yes, dogs go back thousands of years and had to hunt in the wild, often scavenging, eating dead carcasses etc. – (hence the BARF diet) – but that scavenging also entailed vegetables, fruits, grains and even earth! Dogs do not need meat to survive, and it is neither cruel nor unfair to feed them a totally vegetarian or vegan diet.

A dog may have 4 legs and human only 2, but aside from a body totally covered in hair (in most cases!) and a waggy tail, their dietary needs do not differ very much from ours. We can either eat meat and fish, or not. We either choose to eat dairy products, or not. A dog's physiology is the same.

There are a multitude of issues relating to canine health that a vegetarian, vegan, or other variation of a plant based diet may certainly assist, such as skin conditions, digestive disorders or even problems relating to joints and consequent arthritis, one of the most painful and debilitating health conditions that your dog can have. As dogs naturally experience the joy of the outdoor life, anything crippling their mobility can make them miserable.

However, one of the main differences between our dog friends and ourselves is the amount of protein necessary to keep them fit and healthy. Their protein requirements are pro rata greater than ours, so you must ensure that your favourite friend gets enough protein, calcium, Vitamin D in particular, but also a broad range of other nutrients found in various plant based foods

At this point we would like to reiterate that whilst many veterinarians are still sceptical about vegetarian or vegan diets for animals, in no way should you ignore their medical advice regarding serious illnesses, nor the treatment of such illnesses. Work with your vet and explain your reasons for your choices and hope that they give you great advice and support your choices.

One of the wonderful things are the stories that you can read – real life 'doggie stories', not fiction, about how vegetarian/vegan dogs have lived to an incredible age and absolutely thrived on this type of diet. Owners often report that dog's temperaments become even gentler and more lovable (if that's possible!) and that they are even 'cleaner' and more active than ever before. Some even seem to maintain a 'puppy like' face, wiping years of their age – we are sure some humans would like to do the same!

The only word of warning – if you have been feeding your friend on a basically meat-based diet or any other form of more traditional dog food, take a slow approach on switching the diet – any change of diet, just in our human form as well, can result in digestive upsets. It may take a while for your dog to adjust, so introduce the food gradually over a period of a few weeks, until they no longer recognise either the sight or smell of meat based food. Any dog will turn their nose up at a vegetarian/vegan based bowl of food if suddenly presented with it. Persevere, and as soon as they are hungry, they will be in 'the trough' faster than you can imagine.

Another important factor to remember is that in the case of 'canned dog foods' – are you really sure what is in them? In commercial dog foods, up to 50% of the contents are based on 'by-products' and 'meal' which can include almost anything! They could even be chomping on their own 'compatriots', as a lot of canned food contains dogs or cats that have passed away and been gathered up by commercial dog food companies. There are also bacterial, viral and fungal issues as well as many other reasons to feed your dog natural foods.

Another recommendation is that you do your own 'swotting' – research vegetarianism or veganism for your dogs, and weigh up the pros and cons in your own mind. The more knowledgeable you are, the better it is for your dogs.

In the forthcoming chapters, we discuss the various ways of making sure that you provide your dog with the complete range of vitamins and nutrients to make sure they have a long and healthy life, PLUS some good recipes for you to try.

So enjoy the book, and more importantly, make sure your dog enjoys our food!

What are the Pros and Cons of Vegan/Vegetarian Diets?

There is no written scientific evidence that either omnivore diets or vegetarian/vegan diets are preferential – no real proof that either is wrong for your dog.

Adequate macronutrients (protein, fat, carbohydrates) in the correct quantities are the core to feeding your dog, along with vitamins and minerals to assist and provide the full package.

Every animal nutritionist or veterinary practitioner has their own views, but who is so say which ones are right? As long as you consult your practitioner/nutritionist with regard to your own thoughts, ideas and practices and are aware of exactly what you are feeding your dog and its nutritional contents, there should be no real problems for healthy dogs.

There are of course, exceptions. Dogs diagnosed with a specific illness or disease will need a controlled diet that is beneficial to that condition. Again, this is an important discussion to have with your vet. **Under no circumstances, suddenly switch your dog to a vegan or vegetarian diet, just because you read something.** You could be causing more damage to your pet by doing so.

Risk Factor

The main risk of feeding your dog a vegan or vegetarian diet is that you do not supply your dog with enough of the correct nutrients as discussed in this book. You should always take your dog for a check up before making any radical change in dietary ingredients or pattern. There could be an underlying disease that has not completely manifested itself, and by changing diet, this could escalate the condition. All breeds and sizes of dog can be fed a vegetarian diet as long as they are bottom-line healthy before switching or making changes.

Exceptions

As previously stated, newly born puppies need their mother's milk, and should be weaned very gradually to a vegan/vegetarian diet. Equally so, pregnant or nursing mothers should not be changed during either the gestation period, or the post-delivery period. They need to fully recover, just like any human being, and any change in diet could drastically reflect their production and quality of milk and essential nutrients for the tiny puppy. It could also cause a hormone imbalance and possible rejection of the new born pups.

You must discuss with your vet what to feed your dog if they are diagnosed with cancer, liver or kidney disease or heart problems. They may refer you to a nutritionist who will work out an exact plan that benefits those particular diseases. Again, no changes should be made at the drop of a hat.

Benefits

There are many case studies available on the benefits of a vegan/vegetarian diet to dogs suffering with allergies, injuries, arthritis, recurrent gastro-intestinal upsets and small non-life threatening illnesses.

Skin irritations and allergies are often sound reasons for feeding vegetarian or vegan diets. A gradual switch to a non-meat and/or non-dairy diet will often speed up the recovery process.

'Start Low – Go Slow'

We cannot reiterate enough the importance of switching your dog's diet, slowly but surely to avoid any stomach upsets. This also applies to any new supplements you may add on a daily basis. This also provide a 'process of elimination' trial to see what may be affecting your dog, and also what could be causing certain allergies or upsets. Again, this is no different to a Homo sapiens test for allergies. You will also save yourself the problem of tummy upsets by allowing your pet to get accustomed to the new additions or changes.

The Best Dog Bowl Ever!

To achieve the best balance of essential nutrients for your dog, it is important to include a variety of protein, fat and carbohydrates, along with vitamins, fatty acids and minerals – not forgetting, of course, plenty of clean water. These ingredients are vital for the well-being of your pet as well as encouraging their natural growth pattern.

Proteins

Proteins of course are easily obtainable from meat, but if you choose to feed your dog a vegetarian or vegan diet, you must attain this protein from plant based foods or other sources such as eggs, soy, cereal, nuts and seeds (be careful of nuts) as well as vegetables. Green vegetables have a surprisingly high quantity of protein that many people would not realise (90g of broccoli for instance, contains between 3-4g of healthy protein).

Each group of foods contains different amino acids, known as the 'building blocks' of protein. They also vary in quality, so you must always look out for 'digestible proteins'. Good protein intake will assist in muscle growth, cell repair and also an element towards healthy bones.

Vegetarian Protein Sources:

- Legumes (beans, lentils, chickpeas, soy beans, other well cooked beans such as pinto).
- Green leaves, such as cabbage, spinach, broccoli.

- Dairy (small amounts of organic protein sources such as goats milk, natural yogurt, cottage cheese, hard cheese such as cheddar or parmesan). Limit the quantities.
- Free Range Organic Eggs – including feeding raw and ground eggshells (see our information on feeding eggshells).

In the case of vegan protein sources, all legumes are fine, as well as vegetables in general. However, be careful with all dogs on the intake of soy, as this does not always agree with certain dogs.

Carbohydrates

It is often argued by many that dogs do not need carbohydrates as an essential requirement for their health. The main reason for a balance of carbohydrates in your dog's diet is for energy – again, it is argued that a dog can extract the necessary energy factor from protein. But protein is required for other necessities, such as building a strong bodily structure, so in order for that protein to be absorbed for more 'useful' factors in the diet which only protein can achieve, carbohydrates kick in to enforce energy density as well as providing valuable fibre, a healthy stomach and essential phytonutrients that cannot be found in other dog food ingredients (specifically meat).

Vegetarian Carbohydrate Sources:

- Most vegetables – all green and cruciferous vegetables (Brussel sprouts, cabbage, broccoli, spinach, cauliflower, celery, green beans, zucchini.
- Other Vegetables – potato, sweet potato, carrots, pumpkin, squash.
- Grains – rolled oats, brown rice, millet, buckwheat, barley (flakes), rolled oats. Make sure that the grains are well cooked.
- Fruit – must always be ripe, and deseeded if the stones are large (small seeds in strawberries, blueberries etc are fine) as these could harm digestion. Always dispose of large pips and seeds into a bin that your dog cannot attack!!

Fats

Fatty acids can be absorbed from either animal or vegetable sources, but dogs do have a particular requirement for Omega 6 fatty acids, commonly called linoleic acid. Your pets can produce nearly all the required amount of fatty acids within their own bodies, **except for linoleic acid.** Not to be confused, dogs also require linolenic acid (Omega 3). Good sources for these acids are listed below.

Vegetarian Fat Sources

- Fatty acids are an intrinsic part of both human and dog diets – most commonly found in flax seed for dogs, but also in cold pressed oils (olive oil, safflower, sunflower in particular), avocados, coconut. Soybeans are also a good source, and the odd drop of evening primrose oil will also provide a good nutritional source.

Pescetarian dogs benefit from the addition of fish such as salmon, tuna, mackerel etc.

Vitamins and Minerals

Whilst the 'macronutrients' needed in your dog's diet have been talked about, there has to be a constant supply of vitamins and minerals to balance out his or her diet.

Vitamins and minerals are found in most manufactured dog foods, but if you are intent on preparing homemade food for your dogs, you may need to use supplements.

In terms of vitamins, many crucial vitamins are found in normal foods such as fruit and vegetables. The most important vitamins for your dog are:

- Vitamin A – helps to maintain a healthy coat and skin
- Vitamin B12 – plays an important role in intestinal health and brain function.
- Vitamin E – supports the immune system

Many vitamins play many roles in providing a healthy diet for your dog, but do take caution, as overdosing on vitamins, particularly in the form of supplements, can have an adverse effect. Always follow dosage accurately and take into consideration what you are already feeding your dog.

In terms of minerals, again, many of these can be found in everyday foods, particularly legumes, fruits, vegetables, grains (meat also carries a considerable amount of minerals, but this is irrelevant if feeding your dog a vegetarian or vegan diet).

Key minerals to be included in your dog's diet and needed in larger quantities are:

- Calcium
- Chloride
- Magnesium
- Potassium
- Phosphorus
- Sodium
- Sulphur

Trace minerals, which are only needed in smaller quantities are:

- Copper
- Chromium
- Fluorine
- Iodine
- Iron
- Manganese
- Selenium
- Zinc

Whichever diet you feed your dog, there may be a need for supplementation. Veterinary Surgeons are somewhat 'undecided' on this topic, with some very much for, and others against the addition of supplements. Another issue you could discuss with your vet!

Water

Never forget a constant supply of water for your dog. Apart from quenching his thirst, water also rehydrates (very important if you have a particularly active dog), eliminates waste from the body, transports nutrients and regulates their body temperature. If your dog shows signs of excessive thirst however, there could be underlying causes which need to be checked out.

Conclusion

A varied diet of the above foods should provide a great platform from which to feed your dog on a vegetarian or vegan basis. However, the use of certain supplements is recommended in order to complete an excellent and healthy diet for your pet.

Please look at the recommended supplements in our relevant chapter.

Remember, dogs do have requirements for their health, just as we do. Protein, fat, carbohydrates and fresh clean water all provide their own vital aspects to your dog's life.

Vitamins and minerals are needed to keep your pet performing at optimum strength, and can be found generally in plant based ingredients, but can also be provided in synthetic form with the use of supplements.

There are no nutrients that your dog needs that are missing from a vegetarian or vegan diet, or added supplements – your dog does not need meat.

Ask Bramble, the Border collie that lived until the ripe old age of 27! He is not the only dog that proves that veganism/vegetarianism is a healthy diet for dogs! Bluey, the Australian Cattle Dog managed to 'creak' his way to 29, almost 30!

'**Bramble**', lived to the ripe old age of 27

Supplements for Dogs

Being a dog owner or being charged with looking after dogs for a living you will want to give your dog the best nutrition you can. This is obviously a high priority to keep him or her healthy, with a glossy coat, fresh breath and full of vitality! While diet is of paramount importance, sometimes canine friends need supplements, vitamins and minerals to help them stay strong and healthy. However, it's important to understand exactly when as well as what supplements are required.

When to supplement

Your dog could need additional vitamins or minerals because of underlying health problems, recovery after illness or because they are following a specific vegan (no eggs or milk products), lacto-vegetarian (consume milk products) or lacto-ovo vegetarian (eats eggs and milk) diet. If your dog is on a normal diet and considered healthy there should be no need for supplementation as he or she should derive all the vitamins and minerals needed from a good daily diet.

Understanding what vitamins and minerals are good for your dog is important. Never just administer the aforementioned without knowing exactly what they do and why they are needed. Too much of a supplement can be damaging so it's vital to do your research first. Many of us humans supplement our diets so automatically so we believe it is wise to do the same for our pets. However, just as doctors advise us to check what supplements we need, the same should be said for your canine friend. Some are just not necessary and can cause more harm than good to your adored pet. Of course, if your vet has suggested certain products then follow this advice.

Dog food that is bought in supermarkets or pet shops is usually fortified with a balanced variety of vitamins and minerals but dogs fed a home-made diet could benefit from certain supplements. If you fall into the latter category speak to your vet if you have not done so already and find out what your dog may need.

If your dog already eats a healthy diet, by giving extra vitamins or minerals you could harm their health. As an example, overdose on calcium and you could give your dog bone issues. Equally, too much Vitamin D can also harm bones (as it does in humans), cause muscular problems and result in loss of appetite. This is particularly pertinent to larger puppies. Another example would be an excess of Vitamin A as this can cause problems in blood vessels, cause pain in your dog's joints and even make them dehydrated.

Please check with your vet before you start to supplement your canine friend. If you believe your dog is at the beginnings of illness don't think you can combat symptoms without being absolutely sure of what you are doing. Symptoms of illness or ill-health can mean there are other underlying problems rather than just your dog being under the weather. Additionally, some supplements will have ingredients in them that can work against any medication your dog has been prescribed. Supplements are not medicine, they are exactly what their name suggests, meaning they are *additional* to diet.

Which are good supplements to use for your dog?

Certain supplements are great for dogs, as an example, fish oils such as omegas can reduce inflammation and the fatty acids can promote a glossy, healthy looking coat. Additionally, vitamins C and E are often advised for dogs suffering with joint inflammation and even for those with memory problems.

With caution, vitamins can improve your dog's quality of life because used correctly they can help regulate your dog's digestive system, reproductive system, liver and blood etc. as well as protect your dog from unseen environmental problems. They can also help maintain healthy skin, coat, muscles and bones. The truth is, all of us need vitamins, whether animal or human because they are responsible for thousands of different chemical reactions in the body and work with minerals to regulate organs. However, animals as well as humans should derive most of their vitamins from the food they eat unless on a specific diet such as vegan, vegetarian or other.

When looking for a supplement for your pet dog, (after checking with your vet) this is what you should be researching before purchasing:

- Understand any ingredients you should be avoiding that could be harmful to your pet
- Don't give human supplements to dogs, some of the ingredients can seriously disagree with your pet
- Check with your vet any claims on the packet – statements such as alleviating certain diseases
- Check the supplement company has credentials or certification on the label
- If seeking a multi-vitamin look for something containing at least 8 essential vitamins: A, D, E, B-complex and B vitamins

The following vitamins should be given to dogs if they are showing signs of deficiency or their diet means they do not derive all they need from their food:

Vitamin	Deficiency sign	Vitamin is derived from...
A	Night blindness, poor skin, hair	liver, fish, vegetables, dairy, liver oil
E	poor reproductive system, Bowel problems	vegetable oils, nuts, green veg, nuts
D	teeth, rickets	dairy, fish, liver oil, sunshine

K	poor blood clotting	egg yolk, kelp, alfalfa
C	poor healing time, increased susceptibility to illness	vegetables and citrus fruits
B1	poor appetite, loss of nerve, control, general weakness	fruit, vegetables, meat, milk
B2	poor growth, eye problems, heart issues	dairy and meat
B5	loss of hair, diarrhoea, greying coat	meat and veg

If you see any of the aforementioned problems beginning to occur then seek advice from your vet as supplements as well as medication would also be advisable.

If you have a puppy you may well be advised to supplement with a daily multivitamin which will make sure your puppy receives all the vitamins it needs for healthy bones, tissue and general good health. An adult dog that is healthy and not on a specific vegan, vegetarian or other diet shouldn't need a supplement however an older dog tends to absorb less vitamins and minerals through their intestines and loses them when they excrete. Additionally, you shouldn't forget they eat less than a younger dog so may not receive their daily vitamin and mineral requirements. This is where you will need to discuss supplementing their daily diet with your vet.

All dogs, regardless of meat diet, vegan or vegetarian should be taken for a daily walk as the sunshine will help with their intake of Vitamin D – not to mention the superb benefits of physical exercise.

My dog is vegetarian or vegan what should I supplement with?

If your dog is following a vegetarian diet you would be wise to seek advice on supplementing vitamin D, B5, and B2 for example. With a well-supplemented, balanced diet based on whole-foods a dog will thrive as a vegan or vegetarian but these canines will need extra vitamins and minerals.

In a vegan and often a vegetarian dog's diet, often missing are Carnitine and Taurine, which many vets advise adding

Carnitine and Taurine

Unfortunately, feeding your dog with either a vegetarian or vegan diet can result in serious deficiencies of both carnitine and taurine.

Carnitine is a water soluble amino acid substance found in your dog's tissue and a deficiency in this can cause loss of firmness in his or her heart's tissue and therefore a poor heart. Carnitine is found in animal tissue which is why dog's without a meat diet are in danger of his deficiency and long term deficiency can cause a defective immune system.

Taurine is another vital amino acid that if lacking in your canine can cause serious health problems. Taurine is found in poultry, beef, and other animal meat so a vegetarian or vegan dog will find it hard to ensure correct levels are consumed. It plays a huge role in regulating the heartbeat, moving calcium in and out of cells, brain activity and keeping cell membranes stable. It is also used in the body to treat heart failure, diabetes and retina damage.

To supplement with Carnitine will mean a dosage of approximately 250mg per 10lb/4½kg of dog body weight and Taurine with 125mg per 10lb/4½kg of body weight.

Does my dog need a Probiotic?

Probiotics, unlike supplements, can be used for all dogs as they aid digestion and modulate the immune system. They contain short- chain fatty acids (otherwise known as SCFA's) which inhibit the growth of harmful bacteria, treat diarrhoea, irritable bowel and intestinal inflammation. It's also believed that probiotics can help avoid urinary tract infections in your dog. Always follow the label when giving your dog a dosage of probiotic.

To summarize....

In summary, a healthy non-vegetarian/vegan dog on a well-balanced diet should not need supplementing. A probiotic will always benefit as their digestive benefits are excellent.

A dog that is on a vegan, lacto-vegetarian or lacto-ovo vegetarian diet will potentially need supplements in their diet particularly Carnitine and Taurine. Speak to your vet to ascertain exactly what is required. If your vegan dog needs extra help with digestive problems, your vet will be able to prescribe something similar to probiotic without the dairy ingredients. Aging dogs as well as puppies and those recovering from illness or with poor health should benefit from supplementation. This is another discussion to be had with your vet.

Finally if your dog has been advised supplements, please don't keep your dog on these indefinitely as there is no record of the safety of long-term food supplementation in canines.

Fish Oils

There is some debate about whether fish oils are good or bad for your dog, mainly centering around whether it can be toxic or not.

Fish oil certainly does have benefits if given in the correct dosages, and like any other supplement, you are urged to consult your veterinarian and seek their advice on how much to give.

Regardless of diet, fish oils contain EPA and DHA which are Omega-3 fatty acids. There are numerous fish oils on the market which vary in intensity and absorption potential, so again, seeking your vet's advice is paramount.

Proven benefits include, but are not limited to:

- Regulation of the immune system (particularly useful for those dogs that may be suffering from allergies autoimmune diseases)
- Regulating blood pressure
- Improving coat and skin
- Helpful in rheumatoid or arthritic conditions
- Mental development and cognitive skills
- Can add in weight loss where necessary

Please do not rush out and buy 'any old fish oil' that also serves humans – they may contain ingredients that your dog will not respond well to.

Also make sure that when serving the fish oil, that it is still fresh – fish oil can go off very quickly. Purchase the oil in small amounts and keep well stored in the refrigerator.

Coconut Oil

The benefits of coconut oil for dogs have not been 'barked' about for very long, but it can definitely be useful for assisting in many types of ways both internally and externally.

Coconut oil is 90% saturated fats which are mainly MCT's (Medium Chain Triglycerides), and most of the benefits of the oil comes from these. Three acids contained in the oil all have similar properties such as antibacterial, anti-fungal and antiviral – a triple hit in the fight against viral illnesses.

The MCTs are also metabolized easily thus providing energy and body fuel for your dog. For overweight dogs with a thyroid imbalance, coconut oil will assist your dog in losing weight and thereby giving them more energy as opposed to lazing around lethargically!

Coconut oil in general will improve the skin and coat of your dog and speed up any healing process that wounds may need, or indeed, 'dumb down' any allergic reactions. It also has internal benefits such as improving digestion and nutrient absorption, and reducing bad doggy breath!

You would be wise to read up on the full benefits of coconut oil, both for you and for your dog – it is well worth it.

Making Your Own Calcium Supplement

Some of our recipes include our own ready-made supplement!

One of the easiest and most economical ways of making one of the supplements your dog will really benefit from is a calcium supplement, made by grinding eggshells, which you would normally throw away. Caution should be taken though if you use any form of 'ready-made' vegetarian kibble or veggie dry food – this will already contain calcium.

Eggshells contain calcium and an array of other micronutrients such as boron, copper, iron, manganese, magnesium, molybdenum, silicon, sulphur and zinc, among other vital elements.

The make-up of an eggshell (you can use any kind of eggs such as chicken, duck etc, but it is better to use organic eggs) comprises of that similar to bones and teeth, and we all know how strong they have to be! The provenance of the eggshells is very important – otherwise they do not contain the right nutrients.

It is important to wash and drain the eggshells before use and leave the shell as it is, trying not to remove the 'skin-like' membrane inside the shell.

Air-dry the shells thoroughly, upside down on paper towels so that any moisture drains out. Break into pieces and then grind in a coffee or herb grinder so that the mixture is powdered down as far as possible. Alternatively, you can place them in a plastic bag and crush with a rolling pin, but keep crushing until the shells are as fine as possible.

Half a teaspoon of this powder is about 440mg of absorbable calcium, and you would need to supplement this amount for every 1lb of food that you put down for doggie to eat. A whole shell from a medium sized egg is enough for 2 portions of food.

For storage purposes, keep in a jar with an airtight lid (a kilner jar is great for this purpose) and place in a cupboard or larder – not in the fridge! The powdered shells will keep for up to a week.

Power for Puppies!

Whilst discussing dietary care for your babies (!) just a quick word about puppy nutrition.

It is best to start a dog early on a vegetarian or vegan diet, but of course, care has to be taken with the very young dogs or puppies. Nutritional requirements will change throughout a dog's life, with particular attention needed to either end of the dog life-spectrum, i.e., puppies and geriatric dogs – lining their tummies with the right amount of balanced nutrition is imperative, as is taking any illnesses or conditions that may have already occurred in your dog's life.

Puppies need the colostrum contained in their mother's milk shortly after birth, as this provides excellent nutrition and the passive immunity to any potential health dangers. After around 6-12 weeks, they develop their own immunity. It goes without saying that puppies from a vegan or vegetarian mother, are likely to inherit the same food tendencies, making life easier if you are currently feeding your dogs in this way.

After around the first month you can introduce 'vegan or vegetarian foods' to the puppies, best consumed by them in the form resembling 'baby food', as you would your own new born baby. Moistened food, mashed or liquidized is the way to go, until they are completely weaned. It is important to realize that the energy requirements for puppies is probably in the region of double that for adults!

Go Carefully for Geriatrics!

Somewhere between 5 and 7 years old, depending on breed your dog reaches this stage of his or her life, but active dogs often delay this stage until much later, such as 9 or 10. Energy requirements gradually decrease and the need for a high level of protein also decreases. Care does need to be taken and more frequent medical checks with your veterinarian are essential to assure you that your dog is not developing any age-related diseases such as diabetes, heart conditions or renal conditions, as this could greatly affect the diet that you feed them.

Things to Watch Out For

If you are feeding your dog on a home cooked diet, including the recipes we are suggesting, you should have at least a yearly, if not 6-monthly vet check, probably also including blood tests – purely for peace of mind and for you to know that what you are doing is right for your dog.

Checking your dog's general condition on a regular basis is also vital. Watch out for the following, whether your dog is vegan or vegetarian.

- Coat – should be full at all times, not patchy or excessive scratching causes irritated areas.
- Eyes – clean, clear and bright
- Excretion or faeces – normal at all times
- Behavior – no abnormal changes in character
- Activity – no lethargy and normal desire to play and go for walks
- Weight – no dramatic changes up or down in weight – vegan and vegetarian dogs will or should be lean, but not overweight or ribs showing.
- Appetite – no changes in desire for food!
- Thirst – no extraordinary thirst, but this applies at all times on all diets

Doggie Hygiene – Homemade Soaps/Conditioners to Smell Nice!

Not only do homemade dog soaps, shampoos and conditioners smell lovely (more importantly they make pooch smell great!) they are also free of additives and other 'nasties' than over the counter purchases.

Herbs and essentials oils used in the right quantities provide wonderful 'hair care' for Henrietta or Bonzo, and you can relax in the knowledge that you are using the best possible products on your dog's skin and hair.

Whilst shampooing or cleaning your dog, take your time, not just to get them clean, but also to use a bit of 'massage therapy' – it's great for them, and it's really relaxing for you too!

Many soaps and shampoos include 'human-grade' cosmetics and chemicals, that can cause dry skin, irritation and even hair falling out. By making your own, you avoid that stress and also avoid shampoos containing petroleum bi-products and also strong detergents, all of which can be harmful to both inside and outside your dog.

Basic Soap Recipe

The only words of caution when making soap for your dog is to watch out for the 'pH balance' of any ingredients. Every dog has their own skin pH level and it is important to adhere to that. A healthy range is between 6 and 8 on the pH level, so if you aim somewhere in the middle of that, the products will be safe to use on your dog's skin.

Ingredients:

- 4tbsp castile soap, grated (make sure you have totally plain castile)
- 8 fl.oz/250ml apple cider vinegar
- 30fl.oz/1 litre hot water
- 30fl.oz/1 litre vegetable glycerine

Method:

Dissolve the Castile in the hot water, shaking vigorously. Add the apple cider vinegar and glycerine and mix thoroughly, ensuring that the soap has dissolved as best as possible. Pour into a 'squeezy' container and place in you doggie storage cupboard. You will get several dog washes out of this (depending on the size and hairiness of your dog). It lathers really well, and you don't need to use much of it at a time.

Always avoid the eyes, ears, nose and mouth when washing your dog. Clean this area separately with a face flannel or cloth.

Dry Shampoo

We all know that bathing or washing your dog can be a bit of an event, so if you want to give them a quick 'clean and freshen up', try using this dry rub shampoo. Simply take some baking soda in a cup (or if you have a talc shaker or sugar sifter, even better for even sprinkling). Gently rub the baking soda into the coat, then brush out thoroughly. This should also reduce any 'smells' and in some cases the 'pongs' will be completely eradicated!

Herb and Essential Oil-Infused Conditioners

For extra special occasions, (or date night!!) use a herb-infused conditioner or essential oil infused conditioner for that delicious aroma!

You can use fresh herbs from your garden (rosemary is obviously a good one due to its' intense smell) – one healthy rosemary stalk should do. You need approximately 2 tablespoons of the herb, which you then immerse in water and bring to the boil on the cooker. Turn off the heat and leave to infuse for about 10-15 minutes. Remove the rosemary and you will be left with a glorious smelling liquid, which when poured over your dog after a bath and good rinse out, will leave him smelling like an angel! Not only that, the coat will definitely have more of a shine.

We also keep a small selection of essential oils, such as geranium, lavender etc. Due to their strength, just a tiny drop in warm water and a good shake, will make a lovely rinse aid/conditioner for your dog.

Massage Therapy for Dogs

We can all remember that wonderful feeling when healing hands 'hit the spot', and we keep calling for 'more and more', 'up a bit, ah yes, 'down a bit', perfect!

Your precious pup is no different – they adore massages and not only is it therapeutic for both of you, it also gives you the ability to notice changes in your dog's body and structure, feel any 'lumps and bumps' that may appear at any time, so you are totally on top of his physical well-being. Not only that, you will also get on top of his mental wellbeing – canine massage is one of the best things for your dog in terms of rest, relaxation, and rejuvenation. Only ten minutes a day is enough to totally transform your dog's character, attitude and demeanour, as well as lowering both yours as well as your dog's blood pressure! So after a hectic day for both of you, settle into a lovely massage – you as the giver and your dog as the receiver of such attention!

Doggie massage comes in many forms as well as relaxation. It can help:

- Tense and nervous pets
- 'Bitey' pets
- Working dogs – warm up and warm down massages to ease those aching bones and muscles

You may not have the need to treat any one of the above, but a daily massage simply as a maintenance method and as stated, to notice any changes in your dogs body or physiology, is well worth the time for both of you.

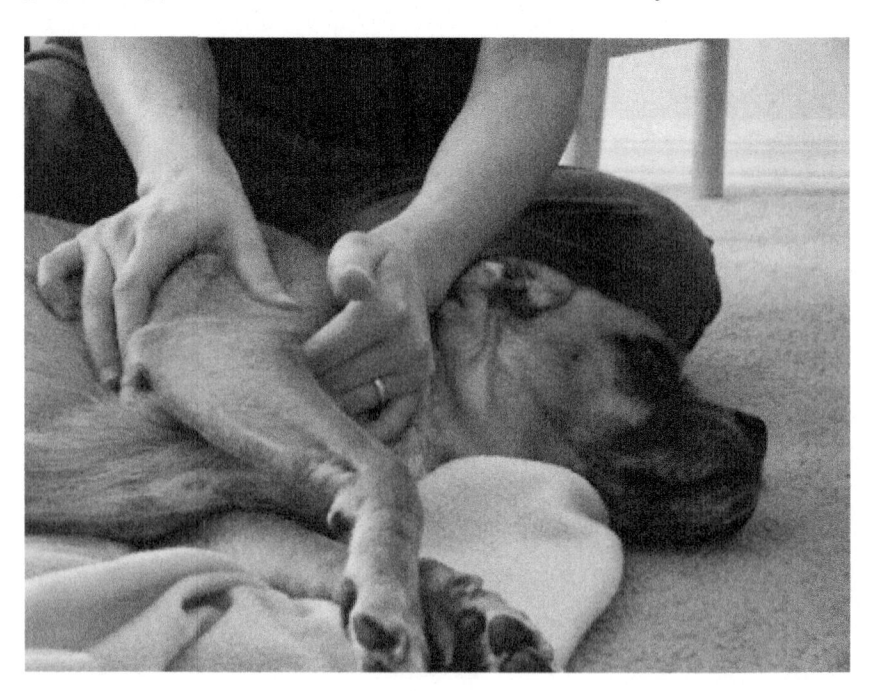

Massage is easy – just work your hands over all of the body, neither gently or with too much pressure, just enough to feel down through the coat to the skin and bones structure. If you dog has any weak points, you will pick this up immediately, either by he or she flinching when touched somewhere, or by noticing something wrong in that area by touch.

Start with long, sweeping strokes from head to tail, for a minute or two – you should feel your dog already beginning to relax. Gently apply a little more pressure, if doggie seems to be enjoying this 'new game'. After a few more minutes, finish with resting one hand at the base of your dog's skull and the other at the top of his pelvis (top of your dog's hips). These are the two 'end points' of the spinal cord, the most sensitive areas that pick up any outer 'fears' that the dog may have, and are the rest and relaxation points for you to finish on. Warm hands, calm and still on these points at the end of the massage, show your dog there is nothing to fear, and that he is loved and protected.

Try it, it really does work!

There are many other forms of canine or doggie massage to treat specific areas, but these tend to be better executed by trained Canine Massage Therapists. If you dog for instance, has weak points due to breakages, accidents etc., special massage is available to pinpoint treat these areas. By trying to do so yourself, you could possibly cause more harm than good.

Care in Making Homemade Doggie Dishes

Achieving the right nutritional balance is not easy, but there are some guidelines to follow. After much research to clearly define what constitutes a 'balanced' meal for your dog, the following parameters are recommended. They are by no means set in stone, and are provided as **a recommendation**, based on your pet's nutritional needs.

Average Size Dog Breed (Labrador, collie) weighing 44lbs (20kg)

Condition of Dog: Healthy, Average Weight, Average Exercise Pattern

Nutritional Information	Amount	Percentage
Serving Size	1lb 2oz/495g	
Total Protein	1¼ oz/32g	16%
Total Carbs	3½oz/100g	58%
Total Fats	1oz/20g	26%
TOTAL CALORIE INTAKE	700g	

Adequate moisture is considered to be around 70% of the total amount of food per serving. Additional vegetables or fruit can be added to enhance the flavor of the dish and to improve the quantity of micronutrients and phytochemicals. Nutritional supplements as outlined in our supplement section will complete all the necessary ingredients for a healthy, well-balanced meal. Many dogs do prefer a more moist diet, so always ensure that you put enough in your dogs meal to maintain their interest in eating.

Classic Kibble Recipe

There are many 'voices' on the subject of kibble, and the 'anti-kibble' movement is yet to be proven. Here is a basic kibble recipe that will contain all your dog's nutritional needs, as well as essential supplements.

Ingredients:

- 1 small/medium sweet potato (approx 2½oz/75g)
- 2oz/55g oatmeal
- 4oz/115g cooked soybeans
- 2½oz/75g cooked lentils
- 1tbsp sunflower oil
- 8oz/225g cooked brown rice or quinoa
- 2tsp ground eggshells*

Supplements:

- Zinc 6g
- L-Carnitine 4g
- Taurine 2g

Method:

Simply mix all the ingredients together using adequate moisture. If preferred, the mix can be baked in the oven for a crunchier texture, if this is what your dog prefers! Add a small quantity of berries or other fruit, or vegetables.

You will need to adjust the balance of this kibble recipe dependent on the size of your dog, age of your dog and physical condition. There is nothing wrong with consulting your veterinarian if in any doubt about your dog's health.

*omit for vegan dogs, but use a calcium supplement instead

Make Your Own Dog Toys and Accessories – Hours of Fun! (?)

Making your own dog toys and accessories has its rewards, when you see how much your doggie loves playing with them – it is not a thankless task – promise! It is probably advisable to limit the use of toys such as this on your new pups – they eat and chew anything and everything, and of course, their teeth and jaws are not fully developed. For the accessories – any age works!

Use 'dog friendly' fabrics, twines and tapes – felt is recommended and also cotton twill tape, as these will not lodge in your dog's tummy – they disintegrate pretty quickly, as does simple cotton.

Don't throw away old clothes such as denims or cotton towels – it is amazing what you can make out of them!

Throw the ball please!

Making your own fairly soft dog ball is easy, and the bonus of this is that it can be thrown in the washing machine if it gets mucky. Here are the simple necessities:

- ✓ 6 pieces of cotton fabric or felt, cut into 'leaf shapes' (you may like to make a paper template to get the right size and shape)
- ✓ Cotton twill tape
- ✓ Strong thread
- ✓ Small scraps of fabric or felt for stuffing

Divide the fabric into two sets of three leaf shapes and stitch together. Stitch the correct length twill tape on to each side of the sets. Sew the two sets together, leaving one side open to stuff the ball with the scraps of material.

Turn the ball inside out and fill with the scraps, then stitch the final opening together. You may like to stitch around the ball again to make it as strong as possible.

Stitch some more twill tape on the top to form a handle, to make it easy to throw – this is just an option. Hours of fun, before you have to make another one!

Note: A close friend took this idea and chopped up some mint leaves and place inside the ball – not only was this a great idea, but the result was nice and fresh doggie breath!

Fetch!

Jute string is a very cheap and natural product that not only makes a very strong toy rope, but also aids in cleaning your dogs teeth.

✓ 1 ball of jute string, cut into 15x22inch/30x45cm lengths.

Lay the lengths of jute string together and secure by tying at one end into a very firm knot. Make sure you have a small tassel at the top, which will be the loose strands.

Put the lengths of jute strings into even groups of 3. Plait the 3 groups together, keeping it as tight as possible along the way. Leave enough string to tie into a tight knot, as at the other end. Enjoy playing!

My Very Own Dog Bowl!

Personalise your dog bowls yourself, as opposed to spending a fortune through companies on the internet.

- ✓ 1 enamel pudding bowl (according to dog size)
- ✓ Masking tape
- ✓ Plastic wrap
- ✓ Blackboard paint or spray (from DIY stores)
- ✓ Chalk or strong stencil for more permanency

Make sure the bowl is scrupulously clean and dry. Mask off the shape you wish to paint, then cover the rest with plastic wrap. Tape down the edges to avoid movement.

Put several coats of blackboard paint, leaving time between each coat for drying.

Remove the tape and plastic wrap when paint is dry. (You can tidy up any scruffy edges of the paint with a craft knife).

Chalk or stencil your dog's name onto the blackboard image.

Next trick – if you have one or more dogs, find a way of making sure they use their 'correct' bowl – you can do this with a bit of trickery!

Frozen Milk Cartons

A bit of fun and goodness for your dog on a hot day.

Take an empty card milk carton and fill it half with water, half with yogurt. Mix a few blueberries through the fluid. Freeze.

When coming back from a hot walk, take the carton out of the freezer and put in the garden. Your dog will love 'sucking' on the carton and, of course, using their teeth to puncture it! Eventually as the carton defrosts, doggie will get to the liquid. You won't be disturbed for a couple of hours whilst they enjoy the delights of the carton!

Our Recipes

We have sorted our recipes into sections to make reference easier for you. Sections are:

- ❖ Vegan
- ❖ Lacto-Vegetarian
- ❖ Lacto-Ovo Vegetarian
- ❖ Pescetarian

However, many of our vegetable recipes that contain eggs, can be used by changing the egg content and using 'flax or chia eggs, and coconut/almond milk can substitute for cot's milk.

The recipe for flax or chia eggs is here in the Vegan section.

Vegan

How To Make Flax or Chia Eggs

There is no need to deprive your vegan dog of delicious baking treats that involve eggs. Simply follow the recipe below and use as a substitute for eggs wherever you need to (obviously certain things do not rise so well, but better to have a great selection of bakery treats for your dog, than not!)

Don't despair that the mixture may look pretty unappetizing to start with!

Serves: Equivalent of 1 medium sized egg.

Ingredients:

- 1 tablespoon ground flax or chia seeds
- 3 tablespoons water

Method:

Whisk together the ground seeds and water until well combined, then place in the fridge to set for 15 minutes.

Use as you would an egg in many of your favorite baking recipes.

Honey and Sweet Potato Cookies

Really good recipe for diabetic dogs.

Sweet potatoes are a great addition to your regular dog treats. They are full of beneficial vitamins such as A, B6 & C.

Consider making these homemade dog treats if you need diabetic dog treats. Sweet potatoes may aid in stabilizing blood sugar and lower insulin resistance, plus they taste great.

Serves: Around 20 cookies

Ingredients:

- 1 large sweet potato
- 3oz/85g apple sauce, unsweetened
- 1 ½ oz/40g honey
- 1 flax egg (or normal egg for non-vegan dogs)
- 4½oz/125g whole wheat flour

Method:

Preheat oven to 350°F/180°C/Gas mark 4.

Peel and cut sweet potato into 1 inch/2cm chunks. Place the potato pieces into a microwave safe bowl, cover with a paper towel and heat for 2 minutes, or until soft.

Mash soft potato chunks with a fork.

Stir together the sweet potato with the applesauce and honey.

Lightly beat the egg (or use flax egg) and stir into the potato mixture.

Gradually stir in the flour until thoroughly combined.

Spray a baking sheet with nonstick cooking spray.

Using a 1 inch/2cm cookie scooper, place rounded mounds onto the prepared baking sheet.

Bake for 20 minutes.

Cool completely on a wire rack before serving.

Store for one week in the fridge or up to 3 months in the freezer.

Pumpkin - You can substitute or mix in fresh or canned pumpkin for this recipe for dog treats. If you use canned pumpkin, be sure that it is pure pumpkin, and not pie filling.

Wheat Free - Make this homemade dog treat wheat free with a wheat and gluten free flour like potato, rice or oat flour.

The soft and chewy texture of this double sweet - sweet potato recipe for dogs really does make them lick their lips!

Apple Bobbers

We call these bobbers, purely because you can see your dog's head 'bobbing' up and down as he enjoys this treat!

Ingredients:

- 3 oz/85g shredded apple
- 3oz/85g almond butter (preferably cold from the fridge)
- 1tsp molasses
- ¼tsp ground flax seed (optional)
- 4½oz/125g whole wheat flour (add 1oz if omitting flax)

Method:

Preheat oven to 350°F/180°C/Gas mark 4.

Shred apples until you have about 3oz apple.

In a food processor with the dough hook attached, add butter, shredded apple and molasses and pulse to combine.

Add flour (and flax seed if using) gradually, about 1oz/28g at a time. Pulse until combined. It will look chunky, but it will come together when kneading by hand.

If you want to avoid greasy hands, put on some latex gloves. Knead dough to bring it together.

Flatten dough onto a piece of parchment or wax paper (less clean-up!) and put another piece of parchment or wax paper between the dough and the roller, then roll out dough to about ¼inch/½cm thickness.

Cut into shapes and place on non-stick baking sheet, or if using parchment paper, just re-use the top layer on the sheet. Even less clean-up!

Bake at 350°F/180°C/Gas mark 4 for 22 minutes, flipping half way through. Turn oven off, and leave treats in warm oven for an additional 5–10 minutes to ensure they are dried out and will have a better shelf life.

Wait till cool, then offer a few to your pup — no doubt he's been watching you like a hawk!

Buster's Best Meatballs

Veggie 'meatballs' can be served as a treat or as a main meal.

Serves: 12 – 20 meatballs (make the balls according to the size of your dog!)
Preparation Time: 10 minutes
Cook Time: 10-15 minutes

Ingredients:

- 2 carrots, grated
- 1 eggplant grated
- 1 clove garlic, minced
- A few splashes water (or skimmed milk for veggie dogs) (you need to judge the amount of liquid when you make the mix)
- 2oz/55g almond butter
- 2fl.oz/60ml water (again, judge the consistency when you are making the meatballs)
- 4 slices whole wheat or whole meal bread
- 1tsp dried rosemary
- A little olive oil for frying

Method:

Pan fry the vegetables and crushed garlic in a little olive oil, until cooked. Leave to cool and then place in a bowl.

Blitz the bread to form a fairly chunky crumb and add to the veg mix. Continue to add the other ingredients a little at a time to achieve the right consistency. Make sure the mix is well combined.

Roll into the size balls that you want. If you are going to serve some that day, cover in plastic wrap and put in the fridge. Freeze the remaining balls for later use.

'Man Come – Mango' Fruit Leathers!

If you were wondering if we had gone totally mad – we haven't! Dogs can eat mangoes, in fact they are good for dogs as they contain and excellent source of Vitamins A, B6 and E, as well as potassium and flavenoids such as beta-carotene. Obviously, like anything else, these should be eaten in moderation. **Please ensure that you dispose of the large seed carefully** somewhere where your dog cannot find it – **the seeds like many fruits contain cyanide.**

Serves: 12-16 good sized strips
Preparation Time: 20 minutes
Cook Time: 4-5 hours in a low oven

Ingredients:

- 3 very large mangoes, peeled, stone removed and cut into chunks
- 2tbsp raw honey (we must not use too much sugar for dogs)
- 1tsp cinnamon
- 2fl.oz to 4fl.oz/60 to 120ml. of water (be careful you only use enough water – you can always thin it out if it is too thick)

Method:

Heat oven to lowest temperature on your cooker. Alternatively, if you have a dehydrator, turn it on to correct setting as per manufacturer.

Put the mango and honey into a saucepan with the water, bring to the boil then turn down to a simmer. Simmer for 10 minutes and check consistency. The mango mix should be a little like jam or thick syrup, so that it doesn't run all over the place when put onto the baking tray. Continue to simmer until you reach that level.

Leave to cool slightly (it will continue to thicken) then mash the ingredients up with a potato masher. Add cinnamon and blitz in the food processor until smooth.

Spread out mango mix on to a baking tray lined with parchment paper as evenly as possible. Bake in the oven for 3-5 hours (depends on your oven!). The leather should be slightly sticky or tacky when you touch it.

Cut into desired amount of strips and roll up. Alternatively, you can make cut-outs in shapes if you want to. Any crispy bits beyond redemption around the sides are still delicious as a snack.

You can eat these too!!

Banana, Carrot and Oatie Bones

Ingredients:

- 11oz/315g whole wheat flour
- 2oz/55g oatmeal
- 4 carrots, grated (squeeze out a little of the carrot juice if very wet)
- 2 large bananas, peeled and mashed
- 1 flax egg (use 1 whole egg for non-vegan dogs)
- 3fl.oz/90ml vegetable oil
- A little raw honey (if desired
- Water – check consistency, about 2fl.oz/60ml or slightly more will suffice

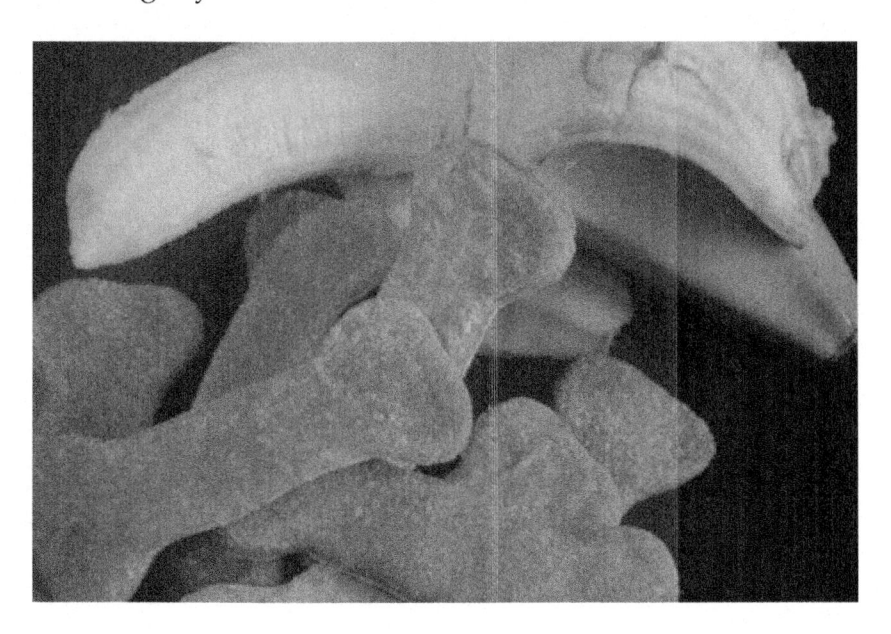

Method:

Preheat oven to 350°F/180°C/Gas mark 4.

Lightly grease one or two baking trays ready for use.

In a large bowl, combine the dry ingredients (flour, oatmeal) thoroughly. In a separate bowl, mix together the wet ingredients (apart from the water). Pour into the dry mix.

Combine together, until they form a dough. Add water as necessary to make it workable, and more importantly to the consistency where you can roll it out.

Roll out dough on a lightly floured surface until about ½inch/1cm thick. Cut out your 'bone shapes' or whichever cutter shape you are using.

Place on the baking tray and bake for 35 minutes. Turn off the oven and leave in the oven to cool and crisp up. The longer in the oven, the crispier they will be. You can leave them up to about 45 minutes – 1 hour.

Delicious Doggie Donuts

Yum, scrum, Mom! Give me more and more!

Ingredients:

Donuts:

- 9oz/250g whole wheat flour
- 16 – 24 fl.oz/475 – 700ml vegetable broth
- 1 flax egg (or flax egg for vegan dogs)
- 3tbsp oats

The following frosting is for non-vegan dogs

Carob Frosting (topping-optional)

- 3 oz/75g carob chips
- 3tbsp butter
- 3 oz/85g honey
- 2fl.oz/60ml milk/soy milk
- 1tsp vanilla

Any topping of your choice (carob chips, mint leaves, parsley, peanuts, anything safe your dog is fond of)

Method:

Donuts:

Preheat oven to 400°F/200°C/Gas mark 6 and line a baking sheet with parchment paper or a silicone baking mat.

Beat egg and in a large bowl, mix with flour and vegetable broth.

Once completely mixed, add oats until all ingredients are combined.

Roll onto a lightly floured surface ½inch/1cm thick.

Use a donut cutter to cut the dough and place on a prepared baking sheet. (If you don't have a donut cutter, just used a biscuit cutter and a small circle cutter to cut out the middles.) Bake for 10 to 15 minutes until browned. Allow to cool and harden.

Once donuts are cool dip the tops of the donuts into the carob frosting and decorate with your topping of choice.

Donuts can be topped with carob drops and dried mint leaves, a little raw honey, or any topping that suits your vegan or vegetarian dog.

<u>*Carob Frosting:*</u>

In a saucepan, combine the ingredients and warm over med-low heat while stirring continuously. Once melted store in fridge

Charlie's Chocolate Drops

These taste quite good, probably you wouldn't eat too many yourself, but they are edible!

Serves: 12 drops (depending how big you make the drops!)

Ingredients:

- 3oz/85g Carob chips
- 2tbsp Coconut Oil
- 2tbsp Peanut Butter
- 2tbsp shredded Coconut

Method:

In a small bowl melt carob chips and coconut oil, stir until smooth. In another bowl mix the peanut butter and shredded together. Fill the bottom of your chosen mold with melted carob.

Top with a small dollop of the peanut butter mixture.

Cover with the rest of the melted carob.

Refrigerate for at least an hour to allow it to set.

Furry Friends Falafels

Ingredients:

- 14oz/400g can chickpeas, rinsed and drained
- 1 garlic clove, chopped
- handful of flat-leaf parsley or curly parsley
- 2tbsp whole wheat flour
- 2tbsp sunflower oil

Please add the Method here

Carrot, Date, and Oatmeal Treats

This recipe covers most things – vegan, gluten free etc! The slight sweetness of the dates will make your dog gobble them up!

Serves: Approx 36 pieces
Preparation Time: 15 minutes
Cook Time: 15 minutes or until dry

Ingredients:

- 7oz/180g gluten-free all-purpose flour
- 2oz/55g instant unsweetened oatmeal
- 2tsp baking powder
- 4oz/115g finely chopped or grated raw carrots
- 2tbsp pitted and finely chopped dates
- 4oz/115g natural unsalted peanut butter
- 4fl.oz/120ml water

Method:

Preheat the oven to 325°F/160°C/Gas mark 3.

In a mixing bowl, combine the flour, oatmeal, and baking powder. Make a well in the center.

Place the carrots and dates in a separate bowl with the peanut butter and water.

Add the peanut butter mix to the well in the flour mix and stir until combined.

Flatten the dough on a lightly floured surface until it is approximately ¼inch/½cm thick. Use a cookie cutter to cut the treats.

Arrange on a cookie sheet lined with parchment paper and bake for 14 to 16 minutes, or until dry.

Let cool for 30 minutes before serving.

Store in the refrigerator for up to 2 weeks.

Blueberry Hummus

Don't think this is made totally as a doggie dish – share this with your dogs, you won't be disappointed, and it's pretty yummy! If you want though, you can add a little tahini paste (about 1tbsp) to make it more authentic, but for you, not for the hounds, as sesame is not one of the ingredients that are 'dog-friendly'

Blending fruits into hummus is a new type of hummus called "frummus". Blueberry hummus is a delicious dip that serves well with fresh fruits.

Ingredients:

- 1 x 16oz/450g can of chickpeas or garbanzo beans
- 16oz/450g of fresh or frozen Blueberry (if frozen, thaw and drain)
- 3-5tbsp lemon juice (depending on taste)
- 2 cloves garlic, crushed
- ½tsp salt
- 1tbsp raw honey
- Warm water

Method:

Drain and rinse chickpeas. Combine ingredients in blender or food processor. Blend for 3-5 minutes on low until thoroughly mixed and smooth. If consistency is too thick, add warm water, 1 tbsp at a time, until desired consistency.

Serve blueberry hummus immediately with fresh, warm or toasted pita bread, or cover and refrigerate. Strawberry hummus is also great served with fresh fruits like bananas, apples, and pears.

Cold Nose, Warm Heart Popsicles

Great for a hot day to cool precious pup down after exercise. Quick and easy to make, keep these in the freezer for that hot occasion. This recipe contains peanuts, which are safe for dogs, but some may have allergies – try a little bit before you feed your dog the whole thing, just to check.

Serves:	**6 small popsicles**
Preparation Time:	**Less than 5 minutes**
Freeze Time:	**Minimum 1 hour**

Ingredients:

- 1 large ripe banana
- 4oz/125g natural peanut butter
- 1oz/25g wheat germ
- 1oz/25g unsalted peanuts, chopped

Method:

Mash the banana well with the peanut butter.

Stir in the wheat germ so that everything is thoroughly combined.

Either roll each popsicle in the peanuts, or mix in the chopped peanuts.

Place in a lidded container and store either in the fridge (if you are going to use straightaway) or in the freezer.

Pups 'Popcorn'

Easy to make, you and your dog can enjoy these together!

Serves: 4 portions
Preparation Time: 10 minutes
Cook Time: About 30 minutes

Ingredients:

- 1lb/450g can chick peas/garbanzo beans*
- ½tbsp light olive oil
- 1tbsp honey
- ½tsp cinnamon
- 1/8tsp sea salt

Method:

Drain and rinse the chickpeas in a colander. Spread them out in between paper towels, pat dry to remove excess water, and then let them further dry for 30 minutes.

In a medium bowl, whisk together the olive oil, cinnamon, and sea salt. Add the chickpeas and coat well. Spread out on a parchment lined baking sheet and bake at 400°F/200°C/Gas mark 6 for 30 minutes, shaking the pan every 10 minutes, until they are golden and crispy. You'll know when they are done because if you taste one it should be crunchy all the way through. If it's still soft in the middle, continue cooking. If you see that they are getting dark, just lower the temperature in your oven and cook them longer. Keep an eye on them after that so they don't burn which can happen quickly.

Remove from the oven, place in a medium bowl and toss with the honey.

Place back in the oven and roast for an additional 6 to 7 minutes to caramelize the honey.

Cool completely.

These can be stored in an airtight container for up to a week, but they don't freeze well. Taste great straight from the oven (for you) and cooled for Henry Hound.

Winter Warmer Vegan Stew

There is no reason why your best friend cannot enjoy some of the wonderful grains available on the market now. You can try quinoa, amaranth or any other grains that you want to experiment with.

Serves: 3-4 portions
Preparation Time: 10 minutes if everything is cooked, 40 minutes if not
Cook Time: 10 minutes with all cooked

Ingredients:

- 1lb/450g cooked amaranth/quinoa or other grain
- 8oz/225g lentils (from a tin, washed and drained)
- 4oz/115g sweet potatoes, cooked
- 4oz/115g cooked leftover vegetables (green beans, carrots, zucchini, spinach etc.)
- 2tbsp vegetarian Omega 3 oil (usually capsules?)
- 8fl.oz/250ml vegetable broth (save from when you cook veggies)

Method:

So easy when everything is cooked!

Place the broth in a stockpot, and put in all the vegetables you want to include, plus the vegetarian Omega 3 oil. Simmer for 10 minutes.

Add the cooked grains and lentils, stir thoroughly and leave to cool. If the mixture begins to dry out, by all means add a little more vegetable stock or water.

Add a little flaxseed or kale chips to the top. Doggie snouts will be straight in the bowl!

Sweet Potato, Almond and Lentil Surprise

Here's a great meat free recipe for your canine friend. It's easy too as once it's made you can keep it refrigerated in portion sizes or freeze and take out when you need it, simply defrost as and when a meal is required. It's nutritious too; making sure your dog gets all his or her vitamins and minerals.

Serves: 2-4 (dependent on dog size)
Preparation Time: 20 minutes
Cook Time: 45 minutes

Ingredients:

- 1½pints/800ml water
- 4oz/115g rice
- 2oz/55g red lentils

- 8oz/225g almond butter
- 1 sweet potato cut into cubes
- 1 potato cut into cubes
- 2tbsp cider apple vinegar
- Small dash of olive oil

Method:

First, boil the water and when simmering, add the rice, lentils and potatoes. Reduce the heat, cover and cook for 45 minutes until everything has softened and the water has reduced. If necessary, add more water if the mixture begins to dry out.

Remove from heat and mash so everything is smooth. Then combine the almond butter and vinegar. Divide into equal servings and refrigerate until required.

Pear and Oat Doggie Biscuits

These biscuits are ideal as a rewarding snack or as a meal and believe it or not, just as good for humans too! They are both tasty and nutritious with the right amount of protein for your pooch.

Serves: 2 (dependent on dog size)
Preparation Time: 20 minutes
Cook Time: 30 minutes

Ingredients:

- 2lb/900g instant oats
- 9oz/250g wheat germ
- 9oz/250g soy powder
- 3oz/85g soy lecithin
- 3oz/85g yeast
- 4fl.oz/120ml olive oil
- 9oz/250g light brown sugar
- 1oz/25g cooked kidney beans
- 1oz/25g cooked pinto beans
- 1 finely chopped pear (make sure ALL the pips are removed)

Method:

Preheat oven to 300°F/150°C/Gas mark 2.

Mix everything together in a blender, then moisten hands and shape into individual patties by rolling and then flattening with your palm.

Place on baking parchment, on a baking tray and bake for 30 minutes. Allow to cool before serving.

Rice and Buckwheat Goodie Tray

This is a delicious dog food recipe for your furry friend and will keep him or her full for a while, plus it's nutritious and gives just the right amount of vitamins, minerals and protein. As an added bonus, there's no cooking time!

Serves:	4 servings (dependent on dog size)
Preparation Time:	15 minutes
Cook Time:	n/a

Ingredients:
- 1½lb/675g cooked brown rice
- 9oz/250g barley (cooked)
- 1lb/450g buckwheat
- 4oz/115g carrot grated
- 4oz/115g eggplant grated
- 1 clove minced garlic
- 1tbsp chopped parsley

Method:

Combine all of the ingredients together into a bowl until evenly mixed and then divide into portions according to your dog size. You can keep in the fridge or freeze for use at a later date.

Quinoa and Almond Butter Yummies

This is a great meal for your dog and is full of vitamins especially vitamins K & C. The almond butter is a good source of protein and the oil will help to give your pooch a shiny, soft coat, plus it's delicious!

Serves: 3 to 4 (dependent on size of dog)
Preparation Time: 20 mins
Cook Time: n/a

Ingredients:

- 9oz/250g quinoa
- 9oz/250g brown rice
- 4oz/115g Kale, finely chopped
- 1tbsp almond butter
- Half a carrot, finely grated

- 1 stick of broccoli finely chopped
- 1tsp basil finely chopped
- Dash of olive oil

Method:

Combine the quinoa, cooked brown rice, kale, broccoli and basil together in a bowl and then mix in the almond butter with a dash of oil until everything is evenly mixed. Portion into containers and store in the fridge.

Tofu and Vegetable Medley

Here is another easy, tasty recipe which is a winner for your canine and is especially good for your dog's liver as it has plenty of anti-oxidant properties and is packed full of nutrients.

Serves: **2 (dependent on size of dog)**
Preparation Time: **15 minutes**
Cook Time: **35-40 minutes**

Ingredients:

- 11fl.oz/320ml water
- 3oz/85g tofu
- 4oz/115g brown rice
- 2 sticks of broccoli finely chopped
- 1 carrot finely chopped

Method:

Prepare the tofu first, by gently sautéing in a pan with a dash of olive oil it will loosen and once cooled you can crumble into pieces. Cook the rice in the water and allow to simmer for 25 minutes. Add the broccoli and carrot for another 10 minutes. Remove from heat and stir in the tofu. Allow to cool and then divide into portions. Serve or refrigerate/freeze portions.

No-Meat Doggie Meatloaf

This is a very special treat for your pooch. This ultimate "meat" loaf (which has no meat) is packed full of goodness, including lots of nutrient-rich vegetables and plenty of protein too. Your dog will be full of tail-wags after sampling this! It refrigerates for days too and it's so good – it's suitable for us humans.

Serves: 4 (dependent on size of dog)
Preparation Time: 20 mins
Cook Time: 90 mins

Ingredients:

- 4oz/115g red lentils
- 12fl.oz/350ml water
- 1½tbsp ground flaxseed
- 1tbsp flaxseed oil
- ½ small eggplant finely chopped
- 1 carrot grated
- 1 celery stalk finely diced
- 3oz/85g oats
- 2oz/55g flour
- ¼tsp garlic powder
- Flax egg (1tbsp flax meal mixed with 3tbsp water)

Method:

Preheat your oven to 350°F/180°C/Gas mark 4.

Rinse the lentils and add 1½fl.oz/680ml of water boil up and simmer for 40 minutes. Give the pot a stir every now and then. Set aside to cool for 15 minutes. In a bowl mix the flaxseed with 1½fl.oz/45ml of water and place in fridge for ten minutes.

Sauté the vegetables in the flaxseed oil for 5 minutes, add the garlic powder. Then blend ¾ of the lentils or mash them firmly with a fork (what to do the other 1/4 lentils?). Mix the vegetables with the lentils; add the oats, flour and flax egg. Finally, place the mixture into a lined loaf tin. Press down the loaf and bake in the oven for 45 minutes.

Serve.

Peanut Butter and Orange Cake

Give your dog a special treat with this peanut butter cake which is not only a delicious dish it's also packed full of good nutrition and healthy ingredients, as well as all your doggy's protein and vitamins.

Serves: 4 to 6 (dependent on size of dog)
Preparation Time: 20 minutes
Cooking Time: 25 minutes

Ingredients:

- 4oz/115g flour
- 4oz/115g whole wheat flour
- 1tsp baking soda
- 2oz/55g peanut butter
- 2fl.oz/60ml vegetable oil
- 2fl.oz/60ml unsweetened honey
- 1fl.oz/25ml orange juice
- 3 medium sized carrots grated
- 1 apple, steamed and pureed
- Flax egg (1tbsp flax meal mixed with 3tbsp water)

Method:

Preheat your oven to 350°F/180°C/Gas mark 4 and grease a 10in/25cm cake tin.

Peel and core the apple (remove all pips) then slice and place in a pan with a little water. On a low heat allow the apple to soften and then puree. Heat the honey and peanut butter on a low heat until it softens and starts to melt. Then mix this with the carrot, apple, vegetable oil, and baking soda, flour and flax egg. Combine until all ingredients are well mixed.

Pour batter into the cake tin and bake for 20 minutes. Use a knife or similar to insert to the centre to check it is cooked through.

Leafy Lentil Loaf

Serves: 8 (dependent on dog size)
Preparation Time: 1 hour
Cooking Time: 45 minutes

Ingredients:

- 2tbsp olive oil
- 1 garlic clove minced
- 6oz/170g broccoli
- 2½oz/70g cooked spinach, cooled
- 2½oz/70g grated carrot
- 2oz/55g breadcrumbs
- 2oz/55g mashed potato
- 2oz/55g red lentils raw
- 2 pints/950ml water

Method:

Preheat oven to 350°F/180°C/Gas mark 4.

Place the lentils into a saucepan with the water and bring to a boil, simmer for 45 minutes and drain. Meanwhile sauté the broccoli with the garlic over a medium heat until they soften and add the lentils, carrot and spinach until everything is combined evenly.

Oil a 9inch/22cm loaf pan and place almost all of the mixture into the tin, saving some for later.

Then in a pan, warm the mashed potato and breadcrumbs and combine. Once everything is nicely mixed, add it to the loaf tin and then cover the top with the reserved lentil mixture.

Bake for 45 minutes until crisp.

Serve warm or cold.

Butternut Squash Muffins

Here's a yummy dog snack which is full of fibre and vitamins and will keep your canine's coat rich and glossy.

Serves: 12 muffins
Preparation Time: 25 minutes
Cooking Time: 15 minutes

Ingredients:

- 2½oz/70g rolled oats
- 2½oz/70g whole wheat flour
- ½tsp nutmeg
- ½tsp ginger
- 1½lb/650g butternut squash cubed
- 1½lb/650g sweet potato cubed
- 2fl.oz/60ml water
- ½ flax egg (½tbsp flax meal mixed with 1½tbsp water)
- 4 fl.oz/250ml soya milk
- ½ tbsp vegetable oil

Method:

Preheat your oven to 350°F/180°C/Gas mark 4 and mix the oats, flour, nutmeg and ginger using a hand-whisk. Peel and cube the butternut squash and sweet potato and place in a saucepan with the water on a low heat – allow to soften. Once it has, mix it with the soy milk, flax egg and vegetable oil in a blender and blend until smooth. Combine with dry ingredients.

Grease and line a muffin tray and scoop one large tbsp of the mixture into each case.

Bake for 15 minutes and allow to cool before taking out.

Butternut Squash and Oat Cookies

Your dog will thank you for these chewy, nutritious and delicious snacks which will keep fresh in an airtight container and jammed full of vital vitamins and minerals.

Serves: 12 cookies
Preparation Time: 15 minutes
Cooking Time: 45 + 15 minutes

Ingredients:

- 1 medium butternut squash
- 2tsp unsweetened honey
- 6oz/170g rolled oats
- ¼tsp ground ginger
- ¼tsp ground cinnamon

Method:

Preheat your oven to 350°F/180°C/Gas mark 4.

Pierce the butternut squash and place on a baking tray, bake for 45 minutes and then remove from oven and allow to cool. Keep oven on!

Remove the skin from the squash and chop the squash, removing the pips. Mash it up and then mix in the oats, honey, ginger and cinnamon. Combine until even.

Moisten fingers and roll into balls (use approximately one tablespoon per cookie) and pat into cookie shapes then place on a greased and lined baking tray. Bake for 15 to 20 minutes and allow to cool before serving.

Carrot and Parsley Cookies

A delicious treat for your dog and the parsley keeps your dog's breath nice and fresh. These treats are packed full of Vitamin A and C. Plus they are so tasty your pooch will be begging for more!

Serves: 24 treats
Preparation Time: 15 minutes
Cooking Time: 20 minutes

Ingredients:

- 1 carrot, grated
- 1tbsp fresh chopped flat leaf parsley
- 6oz/170g dried parsley
- 1lb/450g whole wheat flour
- 1 flax egg (1tbsp flax meal mixed with 3tbsp water)
- 4fl.oz/120ml water

- 2fl.oz/60ml unsweetened honey
- 9oz/250g whole wheat flour

Method:

Preheat oven to 350°F/180°C/Gas mark 4. In a bowl combine the flour, fresh parsley, carrot and dried parsley together. In another bowl mix the flax egg together and then stir in the water and honey. Combine all the ingredients together and place on a greased and lined baking tray. Moisten fingers and form balls from the mixture (using approximately 1tbsp of the mix), then form into flatter cookie shapes. Place on the baking tray and bake for 20 minutes. Allow to cool before serving.

Sweet Potato and Apple Surprises

This is a tasty sweet treat that is good for your canine too. It is full of nutrients, packed with vitamins and minerals and easy to make.

Serves: 10 to 12 servings (dependent on dog size)
Preparation Time: 20 minutes
Cooking Time: 40 + 30 minutes

Ingredients:

- 1 sweet potato
- 3 flax eggs (3tbsp flax meal mixed with 9tbsp water which is 3 x flax eggs)
- 4fl.oz/120ml unsweetened applesauce
- 2fl.oz/60ml unsweetened honey
- ½tsp nutmeg
- ½tsp ginger
- ½tsp cinnamon
- 1lb/450g whole wheat flour
- 8oz/225g rolled oats

Method:

Preheat oven to 350°F/180°C/Gas mark 4 and grease and line a muffin tray. Place the sweet potato on foil and pierce the skin, place in the heated oven then roast for 40 minutes. Allow to cool and then peel off the skin.

Mash the sweet potato and mix with the flax eggs, honey and applesauce. In another bowl mix the cinnamon, nutmeg, ginger, flour and oats. Make a deep hole in the dry ingredients and place the wet ingredients into the middle, then stir together until everything is even. Spoon (1tbsp each) into the muffin tins and bake for half an hour. Allow to cool before serving.

Roasted Vegetables with Applesauce

A yummy concoction of root vegetables and a slight bitter sweet taste of apple, and a kick of ginger.

Lap it up doggie!

Serves: 2 medium sized portions
Preparation Time: 5 minutes
Cook Time: 25 minutes

Ingredients:

- ½ small aubergine, diced into small pieces
- 2 sticks celery, finely diced
- ½ small squash, cut into small cubes
- 2 apples, peeled and diced
- Sprinkle of ground ginger
- Olive oil for roasting

Method:

Heat oven to 400°F/200°C/Gas Mark 6.

Prepare vegetables/fruit as instructed. Place in a roasting tray and toss with a little olive oil. Roast for 25 minutes until tender and apples a little mushy.

Remove the vegetables (only half the apples), sprinkle with ginger and stir around. Crush the other half of the apples to a mash, and place in with the vegetables. Mix around until the moisture is all through the mix.

Pumpkin Cookies

Not only is this a vegan treat for your dogs, it is also gluten free for those suffering with wheat allergy.

Ingredients:

- 14oz/400g rice flour
- 2 flax eggs
- 10oz/250g canned pure pumpkin
- 2oz/55g all natural gluten free peanut butter
- ½tsp ground cinnamon
- ¼tsp ground ginger
- water (about 2fl.oz/60ml, but you may need more)

Method:

Preheat oven to 350°F/180°C/Gas Mark 4.

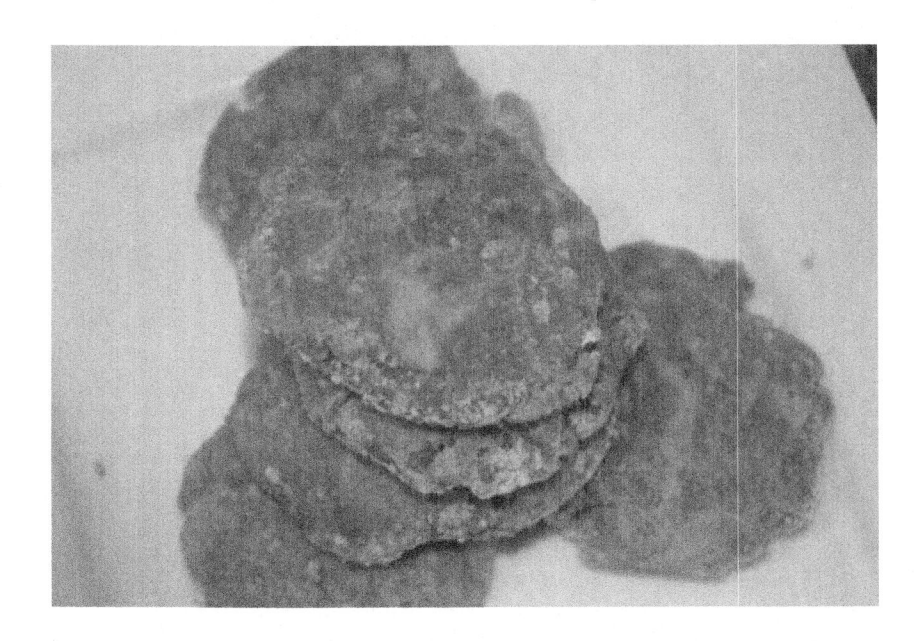

Mix all ingredients together in a large bowl. Be easy with the water, add a little at a time to achieve a dough consistency.

Dust work surface with a little more rice flour and roll out dough until approximately ¼inch/½cm thick.

If you have cookie cutters, use these to cut the dough into shapes for a bit more fun.

Place on a non-stick baking tray and cook for 20-25 minutes. Leave to cool before feeding your hound!

These cookies will keep for about a week in the fridge in an airtight container. You can of course freeze them for up to one month.

Sweet Potato and Parsnip Chews

These are yummy and chewy treats (you can make them crisper by cooking for longer, but they are designed to make your dog use his teeth and help his gums). Use a food hydrator if you have one, if not, follow the instructions for your oven.

Serves: Approx 16 chews
Preparation Time: 15 minutes
Cook Time: 3 hours plus

Ingredients:

- 2 Large Sweet Potato, washed & dried
- 2 large parsnips, peeled
- A little oil to brush (don't overdo it)

Method:

Preheat oven to 250° F/125°C/Gas Mark 2

Line a baking sheet with parchment paper.

Cut off one side of the sweet potato, top and tail the parsnip lengthwise, as close to the edge as possible. If you have a mandolin, you can cut thinner slices. Cutting the side of the potato first allows you to then turn the potato onto this flat surface to make it more stable.

Cut the rest of the potato/parsnnip into 1/3"/1cm slices, no smaller than 1/4"/1.2cm.

Place them on the prepared baking sheet.

Bake for 3 hours, turning half way through.

Cool completely on a wire rack.

Although these treats are dried, you will want to keep them in the refrigerator for up to 3 weeks. You can freeze them for up to 4 months.

Degree of Chewiness - Baking for 3 hours results in a soft, but chewy dog treat. If your dog prefers more of a *crunch*, then bake for an additional 20-30 minutes. When you take the sweet potatoes out of the oven, they may at first appear to be too soft. Let them cool completely on a wire rack before you decide whether or not to bake them longer. This is because they will continue to dry or harden while cooling.

Finished Color of Treat - Sweet potatoes can vary in flesh color when raw. So, when baked they can be lighter or darker than the chews in the above photo. The texture is what you need to be most concerned with. Bake longer or shorter for the texture that your dog prefers.

Carrot Pate

This is quite a delicious pate for both adults and dogs. It will keep in the fridge for up to 5 days, so have a little bit on a cracker (for you) and one of our tasty dog biscuits (for the furry fellows).!

Serves: 1 medium sized bowl for both of you
Preparation Time: 5 minutes
Cook Time: 50 minutes

Ingredients:

- 6oz carrot, in chunks
- 1 clove garlic, whole
- 1-2 tsp olive oil
- 2oz chick peas from a can, washed and drained
- ½ tsp apple cider vinegar (known to lower blood sugar in dogs and adults!)
- 1tsp honey
- Pinch nutmeg

Method:

Wrap the carrot with the garlic clove and olive oil inside a piece of aluminium foil. Roast in the oven for 45-50 minutes.

Place into a blender or processor with the chick peas, vinegar, nutmeg and honey and any oil from the parcel.

Blitz until smooth, place in a bowl ready for serving that delicious snack for that moment when it's just you and the dog!

Doggie Kale Chips

Ingredients:

- 1 bunch of curly kale
- 1tbsp olive oil
- 1tsp salt
- ½tsp fresh ground pepper

Method:

Pre-heat the oven to 300°F/150°C/Gas mark 2.

Rinse kale leaves and dry thoroughly, using a paper towel to pat away any excess water. Gently rip each leaf away from the stem and break into 2inch/4cm wide pieces. Add to a large bowl and drizzle with olive oil. Sprinkle with salt, pepper (curry powder, optional) and toss to coat, ensuring each leave is oiled up well.

Spread kale leaves evenly in a single layer on a non-insulated baking sheet (rack optional, but recommended). Pop in the oven and bake for a total of 15 minutes, in 8 minute increments. Remove from the oven once the leaves have darkened and are crisp. Allow chips to cool on the tray for 2 minutes before devouring!

Lacto Vegetarian Dogs

Blueberry Cobbler

Blueberries are a fantastic addition to your dog's diet with copious amounts of dietary fibre, antioxidants and Vitamins C and E. Antioxidants particularly show great effect in dogs suffering from cognitive disfunction problems and assist greatly in boosting the immune system.

Serves: 10-15 cobblers
Preparation Time: 10 minutes
Cook Time: 25-30 minutes

Ingredients:

- 6oz/170g wholemeal flour
- 4oz/115g oatmeal
- 5fl.oz/150ml milk (moved to this section because milk not vegan)
- 2oz/55g apples, peeled and chopped

- 3oz/85g blueberries, chopped

Method:

Heat oven to 350°F/180°C/Gas mark 4.

Grease a cookie sheet with a little olive oil or butter.

Mix together all the ingredients thoroughly to form a rollable dough. Lightly flour your hands and form the dough into balls (use whichever size you need for your dog – remember, this is a treat, not a main meal).

Place on the cookie sheet and bake for 25-30 minutes if large, or 10-15 minutes if the dough balls are quite small.

Remove from the oven and leave to cool before serving.

'Sausage and Mash' – Share this with Your Dogs!!

Not really sausages, but sausages known as 'Glamorgan' you make yourself, without all the horrible additives. We seriously mean make this for the family and for the doggies! This recipe is packed with protein, which will strengthen your dog's muscles and give them plenty of energy.

Serves:	20 small sausages (about 2 ½ inches/5cm)
Preparation Time:	5 minutes
Cook Time:	20 minutes

Ingredients:

- 4 carrots, grated
- 2tbsp strong cheese such as Cheddar
- 2tbsp parmesan cheese (freshly grated)
- Small handful fresh parsley, chopped
- 4 oz/100g sweet potato, mashed (you could use the equivalent amount of breadcrumbs)
-
- A little olive oil for greasing
- Dusting of flour

Method:

Heat oven to 350°F/180°C/Gas Mark 4.

Mix all the ingredients together in a bowl. Using your hands, form into small sausage shapes.

Place on the greased baking tray and cook for 20-25 minutes. Serve when cool, freeze the rest for up to one month.

You could eat these with a mustard or tomato dip – yum!

Cheesy Feet Bikkies

Ingredients:

- 9oz/250g whole wheat or rye flour
- 7oz/200g shredded cheddar cheese (if you want them 'cheesier' substitute a little of the cheddar for grated parmesan)
- 2 fl.oz/60ml olive oil
- 2fl.oz/60ml water
- 1tbsp flaxseed

Method:

Preheat oven 350°F/180°C/Gas Mark 4.

Mix the flour, cheese and oil and flaxseed together in a bowl blending well.

Add water slowly until it forms a dough like consistency and you would be able to roll it out.

Flour your work surface. Roll dough out as thin as possible (makes the 'cheesy feet' crisper!) We have used a 'foot cutter' but you can use whatever cutters you have to make different shapes.

Place on cookie sheets and bake for 10 minutes.

Turn off the heat and leave in the oven to make them really crispy.

Store in an airtight container, to retain crispness.

Doggata Frittata (Kale)

Ingredients:

- one medium bunch of green or purple kale (about 8 leaves), chopped into small, bite-sized pieces
- splash of olive oil
- pinch of sea salt
- 6 eggs
- 2½fl.oz/80ml milk
- 2oz/55g shredded cheese (recommended: Cheddar and some Parmesan)

Method:

Preheat oven to 400°F/200°C/Gas mark 6. Grease the cups of a standard 12-muffin tin. Sauté chopped kale in a large skillet, preferably cast iron, with a splash of olive oil and pinch of salt. Cook, stirring often, for about 5 minutes, until the kale is tender, dark green and fragrant. Set the kale aside to cool.

In a medium mixing bowl, whisk together the eggs and milk. Stir in the cheese and kale. Use a large spoon to transfer the mixture into each of the muffin cups, filling them about halfway. Bake for 18 minutes, or until the frittatas are lightly golden.

Store in the refrigerator, covered, for up to 3 days. Use organic ingredients if possible. If you'd like smaller frittatas, try filling the muffins cups about a quarter of the way, and check for doneness after 8 minutes.

All Day Breakfast Veggie Style

Lovely healthy recipe for pet pooch – simple ingredients and very cost effective, whilst giving them the nourishment that they need.

Serves: 1
Preparation Time: Less than 5 minutes
Cook Time: Less than 5 minutes

Ingredients:

- 1 egg
- Handful of baby spinach, shredded
- 1 medium sweet potato, peeled cubed and boiled
- ½tsp kelp powder
- Drizzle of olive oil

Method:

Shred the spinach and set aside – it is best to shred it finely.

If you haven't already got a sweet potato cooked, peel and cube a potato and boil in water for approximately 10 minutes until tender.

Fry the egg in a tiny amount of olive oil. When cooked, leave to one side.

Place the shredded spinach and sweet potato cubes into the same pan, and cook until the potato is warmed through slightly and the spinach wilted.

Place in your dog's food bowl, sprinkle with kelp powder and serve with our granola bar (see recipe), either crumbled over the top or as an 'after'!!

Snowman Frozen Fruit Treats

A bit of anomaly- because they are white and a great treat for after Christmas lunch, they are also well served to your dogs on a hot day! So simple but so enjoyable a treat for pups and even older dogs.

Serves: 8
Preparation Time: Less than 5 minutes
Cook Time: No cook!

Ingredients:

- 7oz/200g Greek Yogurt (or fat free yogurt if you prefer)
- 1tsp coconut oil
- Handful of fresh blueberries, chopped

Method:

Mix the yogurt, blueberries and coconut oil together until thoroughly combined.

Use an ice tray or mini domes to shape the treats.

Freeze for 2 hours or more, before popping one out as a luscious doggie treat!

Pooch Pizzas

Why should you leave your other member of the family out, when you tuck into pizzas? Have great fun making these mini pizzas (the base can also be eaten by humans!) So, experiment with toppings for your dog and see how much enjoyment you both get out of them!

Serves: 8-10 mini pizzas
Preparation Time: 20 minutes
Cook Time: Maximum 15 minutes

Ingredients:

For the Crust:

- 9oz/250g whole wheat flour
- 1tsp dried basil
- 1tsp dried oregano
- 1 egg
- 2fl.oz/60ml low fat milk
- 4fl.oz/120ml water
- Extra flour for dusting

Method:

Heat oven to 350°F/180°C/Gas mark 4.

Mix together the flour, basil and oregano. In a separate bowl, whisk the egg and mix in the water and milk.

Just as you would making pastry for yourself, make a small well in the centre of the flour mix and pour in the wet mix.

Mix thoroughly to combine, trying to get rid of any lumps.

Remove from the bowl and knead into a firm dough. If a little sticky, add a little more flour.

Roll out the dough on a floured surface to approximately ½inch/1cm thick. Cut into small circles with a biscuit cutter, or make into 2 or 3 larger pizzas that you can slice or cut into bits when cooked.

Top with a green bean puree, a pea and mint puree, or a sweet potato puree to use as your sauce. Finish off the pizzas with vegetables of your choice, and finally top with grated cheese such as cheddar and a dash of parmesan.

Bake in the oven for up to 15 minutes maximum – you be the judge.

Note: You can use tomato puree (unsweetened). We have merely suggested the alternative 'sauces' as many people

don't like to feed their dogs tomato in any form. REMEMBER – it is the stalk of the tomato that can cause tummy upsets, not the flesh.

Lacto Ovo Vegetarian

Eggy Macaroni Cheese Bake

This will fill your pet up quite easily when on this kind of diet. You can make it as 'cheesy' as you like, try combining different cheeses and herbs to give it a really savoury flavour.

Serves: 4 large portions (be careful as you don't want a podgy pooch)
Preparation Time: 10 minutes
Cook Time: 30 minutes in total

Ingredients:

- 4oz/115g cooked whole wheat pasta (as per manufacturer's instructions
- ½ pint/280ml milk
- 1tbsp flour
- 1 egg beaten, plus egg shell, crushed
- Small handful fresh rosemary, chopped
- 4oz/115g cheese (mix of cheddar and parmesan) grated
- 1tbsp butter

Method:

Cook pasta as per packet instructions, drain and set aside.

Make a roux by melting the butter in a pan and stirring in the flour. Add the milk and continue to stir until the roux thickens. Add ¾ of the cheese and stir until melted and smooth.

Put the pasta into a bowl and mix in the beaten egg, eggshell and sauce.

Pour into a baking dish, top with remaining cheese and herbs.

Bake in the oven for 20-25 minutes until firm and set. The top should be crispy.

Leave to cool and cut into 'dog size' portions (depending on size of your dog).

Serve with cooked vegetables, or break into pieces as a treat.

Porridge

Serves: 2 – 4 portions, depending on size of dog

Preparation Time: 10-15 minutes (including cooking)

Ingredients:

- 20fl.oz/600ml water
- 5oz/125g old-fashioned porridge oats
- Finely ground eggshells (you judge the amount that your dog will eat)
- 1 small grated carrot
- 1 small grated courgette
- ½tbsp finely chopped fresh parsley
- ½tsp finely chopped fresh rosemary
- Dash of olive oil
- Dash of milk (up to you, depending how milky you want it)

Method:

Bring water to the boil, then add the oats. Cover the pot and leave to sit for up to 10 minutes. Do not stir, it will make the porridge very mushy

Pour into a dish and add the remaining ingredients. Stir thoroughly.

Leave to cool before serving.

You could add a small chopped banana instead if you wish

Kedgie-Veggie

A take on Kedgeree but without the fish, this is ideal for lacto-ovo vegetarian dogs. If you are not keen on giving your dog brown rice, you can substitute for cooked oatmeal.

Serves: **2-3 medium sized portions**
Preparation Time: **5 minutes**
Cook Time: **15-20 minutes**

Ingredients:

- 1lb/500g cooked brown rice (or oatmeal)
- 1tbsp nutritional yeast
- 4tbsp whole milk
- 2oz/55g grated cheese
- 1 small carrot, grated
- ½ small courgette, grated

- 3oz/85g cottage cheese
- Extra vegetables to hand (cabbage, asparagus, spinach, kale, sweet potatoes, beets – all cooked)

Method:

Heat oven to 350°F/180°C/Gas mark 4.

Use a casserole dish and layer the vegetables and rice throughout along with the cottage cheese.

Pour the milk over the top. Sprinkle with cheese and bake in the oven for 15-20 minutes until the top has browned lightly and bubbling.

Doggie Scotch Eggs

A lovely little recipe that you will enjoy as well! Have a quick bit of lunch or snack with your canine friend, or takes these delicious eggs on a picnic – you will both gobble them up after a run round the park!

Serves: 6 Scotch Eggs
Preparation Time: 30 minutes
Cook Time: 20 minutes

Ingredients:

- 7 large eggs
- 1tbsp olive oil, plus extra for rolling
- 2 garlic cloves, crushed
- 1 tbsp dried mixed herbs
- 14oz/400g can chickpeas, drained
- ½ small pack parsley, leaves only
- 7oz/200g wholemeal breadcrumbs
- 5tbsp wholemeal flour, plus extra for dusting
- 1oz/30g panko or dried breadcrumbs
- 3tbsp ground pumpkin or sunflower seeds(grind them in your processor or coffee grinder)

Method:

Boil the eggs for 8-9 minutes until set. Remove shells and leave to cool before handling.

While the eggs are cooling, gently 'sweat' off the garlic, then add the dried mixed herbs, stirring to mix together.

Place the mix into a processor, and add the chickpeas, breadcrumbs and fresh parsley. Blitz until you have a paste, but not a thin paste. Stir in the wholemeal breadcrumbs and flour and remaining egg, pulse for a few seconds until mixed together.

Take each hardboiled egg separately and using your hands, wrap some of the mixture around each one until the egg is completely covered. Dust each one with a little flour and then the panko or dried breadcrumbs and finally the ground seeds. (You can mix the seeds with the flour first if preferred).

Bake in the oven for 20 minutes at 350°F/180°C/Gas Mark 4 until firm to the touch. Leave to cool before putting in an airtight container.

Luxury Lacto Lasagne

A lovely alternative to a meat lasagne, and both you and your dog will lap this up!

Serves: 2 medium portions
Preparation Time: 20 minutes
Cook Time: 25-30 minutes

Ingredients:

- 6 dried lasagna sheets (preferably spinach lasagne)
- 1 tbsp olive oil
- 6 baby courgettes, washed trimmed and finely sliced
- 1 fat clove garlic, peeled and crushed
- Handful baby spinach, blanched in hot water
- 250g tub of ricotta cheese
- 50g strong cheddar cheese, grated
- 1tsp dried mixed herbs

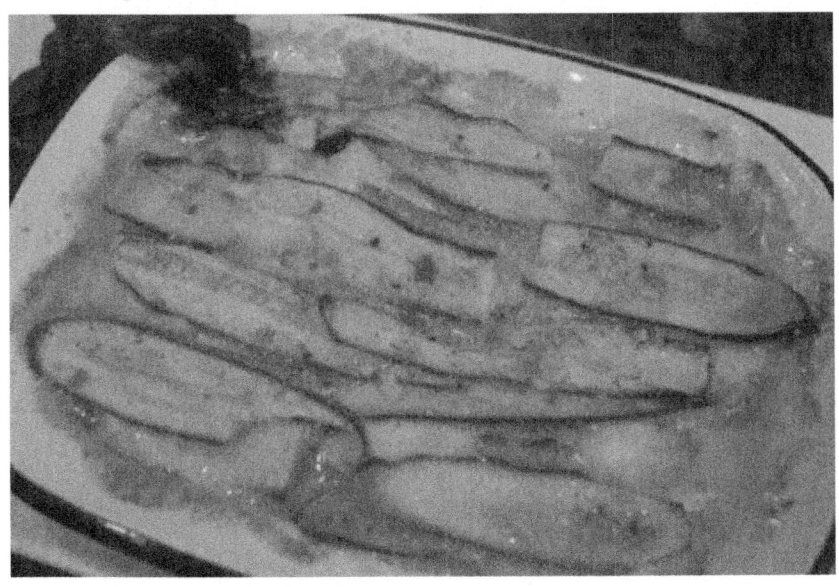

Method:

So simple – heat oven to 350°F/180°C/Gas Mark 6.

Prepare the courgettes and spinach as determined and set aside.

Mix the crushed garlic in with the ricotta cheese and dried herbs.

Start with a little of the cheese sauce, then layer up the pasta sheets with the spinach and courgettes alternately. After each layer, add a little cheese sauce.

Finish the top with a layer of courgettes and a sprinkling of herbs – simple!

Bake in the oven for 25-30 minutes, leave to cool enough so as not to burn doggie's mouth.

Egg and Sweet Potato Rice

Eggs are good for dogs as they contain Vitamins B and E as well as phosphorus. They also contain protein and fat (most of the fat is found in the yolk. If you are trying to keep the fat content down on your dog, use 4 egg whites to 1 yolk.

Serves: 3-4 portions
Preparation Time: 5 minutes
Cook Time: 10-20 minutes (you may already have some cooked brown rice)

Ingredients:

- 2 medium sized sweet potatoes, peeled and diced
- 4 eggs
- Large handful baby spinach
- 8oz/225g cooked brown rice
- 1 carrot, grated

Method:

Cook the potatoes until they are tender, drain and place in a bowl.

Mix in the brown rice and grated carrot.

Place the spinach in a colander and pour over some hot water to soften. Drain thoroughly.

Mix the spinach into the bowl with the rice, potatoes and carrot. Set aside.

Beat the eggs and place in a microwaveable bowl. Microwave, stirring once, until completely cooked. Tip the eggs into the already prepared mixture.

Mix thoroughly and serve when cool enough for doggie to digest.

Broccoli Mimosa

A delicious Lacto-Ovo recipe, combining cottage cheese, herbs, broccoli and grated egg. We think 30 seconds in the bowl before it is clean!

Serves: 1 medium sized portion
Preparation Time: 5 minutes
Cook Time: 10 minutes

Ingredients:

- 4 pieces of tender stemmed broccoli, cooked and chopped (easy on the stalks)
- 1 egg, hardboiled and grated
- 7oz/200g plain cottage cheese
- Small handful mint leaves, finely chopped

Method:

Once cooked, mix together the broccoli, egg, cottage cheese and mint.

Sprinkle with a little more chopped mint to get the 'snifflers' going!

You will definitely see a clean bowl!

Pescetarian

Cod, Pea and Mint Bites

Serves:
Preparation Time: minutes
Cook Time: minutes

Ingredients:

- 3 large sweet potatoes, peeled and cut into chunks
- 12oz/350g cod or haddock fillet
- 4oz/115g frozen peas
- 1oz/30g whole wheat flour
- 1 large egg, beaten
- Handful mint leaves, finely chopped

Sardine and Tomato Triangles

Little pastry triangles with dog-adored sardines- we have made these with canned sardines in tomato sauce, but you can make them with sardines in olive oil.

Serves: Makes 30-40 snack biscuits
Preparation Time: 5 minutes
Cook Time: 30-40 minutes

Ingredients:

- 1 x 4oz/115g tin of sardines in tomato sauce or oil.
- 1 egg
- 1tbsp (heaped) of dry porridge oats or oatmeal
- 5-7tbsp (heaped) rice flour.

Regular plain flour can be used if you prefer, however rice flour ensures that the treats are suitable for dogs with a wheat or gluten intolerance.

Method:

First you need to preheat the oven to 300°F/150°C/Gas mark 2.

Put the sardines in a large bowl and mash with a fork.

Beat the egg and stir into the sardines.

Stir in the porridge oats.

Add the flour 1tbsp at a time and mix until you reach a soft dough like consistency that you can roll out. You may need a little more or a little less flour, so be careful to get the consistency right.

Bake in the oven for 30-40 minutes until golden and firm to the touch. Leave to cool before serving or putting in a tight-lidded container.

You can also use these with our Blueberry Hummus – try them – doggie will love the fish and fruity tastes!

Mackerel Scramble

This recipe is quick and simple if you use tinned mackerel fillets or completely deboned mackerel fillets cooked from fresh, then you will not have to go through the process of picking out any harmful bones that may get stuck when your doggie is eating.

Serves: 2 small portions (depending on size of dog)
Preparation Time: Less than 5 minutes
Cook Time: 5 minutes

Ingredients:

- 2 eggs
- 1tbsp milk
- 1 small can mackerel fillets in olive oil (or 1 mackerel fillet cooked in foil for 10 minutes in the oven)
- Small zucchini, grated

Method:

Beat the eggs and milk together.

Dry fry the mix in a non-stick pan, adding the zucchini as soon as the egg starts to set.

Half way through, add the mackerel fillets with a little of the oil from the can. Continue to stir until the mix is light and fluffy.

Leave to cool before serving to your dog – slightly warm is fine, but certainly not at the temperature you or we would eat them!

Salmon and Veggie Patties

Serving? Prep and cook time?

Ingredients:

- 1oz/25g coarsely chopped green beans
- 1oz/25g coarsely chopped sweet potatoes
- 1oz/25g coarsely chopped zucchini
- 1oz/25g coarsely chopped yellow squash
- 4 fl.oz/125ml water
- 8oz/225g salmon
- 1tsp grated Parmesan cheese
- 2tsp plain yogurt

Method:

Combine the green beans, sweet potatoes, zucchini, yellow squash, and water in a large skillet over medium heat.

Bring to a boil, then add the salmon.

Cover and steam for 5 minutes, or until the fish flakes easily when tested with a fork.

Add the orange juice (not listed under ingredients so please add), parmesan cheese and the yogurt and blend well.

Shape into patties and either serve right away or store in the refrigerator. Freeze any portions you won't use within 2 to 3 days.

Tonno e Fagioli

This recipe is especially good for dogs who have skin allergies to improve coat condition and also really healthy for older dogs with joint problems.

Serves: 4 portions (medium sized)
Preparation Time: 15 minutes
Cook Time: 15 minutes

Ingredients:

- 6 x 4oz/115g cans tuna in oil
- 6oz/170g pasta (wholewheat or gluten free for dogs with allergies)
- 1 large apple, lightly softened
- 4oz/115g pinto or navy beans
- 4oz/115g green beans, cooked and sliced into small pieces

- 6oz/170g yogurt
- Fresh mint or parsley

Method:

Cook pasta according to package instructions. Wash and drain the canned beans

Slice and cook carrots until softened. In blender add cooked carrots and yogurt and blend till smooth.

Mix and fold together the tuna, apples, beans, pasta with green beans and yogurt

Serve with fresh mint or parsley.

Simple Home Remedies for Precious Pup/Daily Dog Problems

As much as we look after our dogs, they will always pick up little allergies, infections or day to day wear and tear when they go scuffling through bushes on their walks! Here are some simple tricks for home cures and soothers before paying out on expensive lotions and potions from your veterinary surgeon.

However, DON'T MAKE THE MISTAKE of not taking your precious hound to the vets when you suspect there is something wrong – our dogs are like our children, they just can't speak, but we know when something is amiss that needs medical attention.

Most of these suggestions you will either have around the house, or can buy relatively cheaply and easily at your local shopping centre. All the better when something simple is making your dog miserable.

Here is a list of suggestions, using those items that you can probably put your hand to straight away.

Brewer's Yeast

- ❖ For some reason, Brewer's Yeast and fleas do not get on! A small dose of Brewer's Yeast in dry food on a daily basis will repel these little biters. If you can add a little garlic as well, the fleas will be running for the hills!

Camomile Tea

- Do you like a cup of soothing camomile tea yourself? If so, let doggie join in – camomile tea bags are great both internally and externally. Camomile tea can soothe an upset tummy in both humans and dogs and is actually recommended by veterinary surgeons. For minor skin irritations, which all our dogs have from time to time, make up a mix of camomile tea and place in a dispenser or squeezy bottle in the fridge. Spray on raw skin or any sore area and it will have an immediately soothing effect. It is a little bit of a magic potion but the tea packs a punch in killing bacteria on the skin – why? No idea, but it works! Before you throw away the tea bag that you have just made your camomile tea with, think again – you can use this to wipe around your dog's eyes. It will soothe the area if it is irritated in any way. Marvellous stuff!

Canned Pumpkin

- If doggie is constipated and appears to be straining, canned pumpkin is a good aid to relieving that 'bunged up' feeling. When dogs are constipated it really shows – they are not good in hiding their feelings!

Citrus Fruits

- Another one for those darn fleas! Fleas are repelled by lemons or even oranges, and probably limes, but haven't tried those yet! Use some fresh lemon or orange juice (squeezed) mixed with water in a spray, and gently spray the surface of your dogs coat. You can also spray your carpets with it. If you want to be really clever, boil some lemons in water and leave overnight – this is even more effective in ridding fleas from your house. However, it is essential at all times that you keep dog towels, blankets and also your carpets (and furniture if you allow pooch on the sofa!) clean as much as possible – they are natural breeding grounds.

Dry and Cracked Paws

- Dogs have cracked paws for a variety of reasons, the most simple of which is excessive use on rough terrain or climatic conditions such as heavy snow or icy conditions.
- In other cases, the condition of paws can be affected by a zinc deficiency in the body. If this is the case, try adding Omega 3 fish oils to daily food intake, which should help the problem. In bad cases of cracked paws, particularly if they become infected, consult your veterinarian immediately.
- Your dogs paws can also react to chemicals used in detergents such as floor cleaners, or those used in fertilizers for outdoor lawns. You will only be able to determine this by process of elimination.
- Pay particularly attention to keeping paws clean, particularly the area between the toes – keep this trimmed of excess hair which harbours bacteria.

- ❖ Of course, you can resort to dog 'boots' – your dog may lose his or her street 'cred', but it could solve any ongoing problems.

Epsom Salts

- ❖ A great soother for bumps and bruises, small cuts and wounds when they are enjoying every sniffing experience in the woods or fields when you walk them! Use an Epsom Salt soak for simple wounds or strains, just like you would have a warm bath to ease your own body. If there is any sign of infection, consult your vet immediately. In the meantime, your pooch will enjoy luxuriating in a warm and healing bath! Perhaps bathing your dog is not always convenient, so you can always use a clean towel, soaked in the warm soak solution and wrapped like a heat pack around the affected area. Bound to put a smile on his or her face, or a welcome lick!
- ❖ Another bonus point is that 'pesky' fleas hate water! Quite frequently this warm bath soak solution will rid your dog of these nasty creatures as well

Natural Essential Oils

- ❖ If you love aromatherapy baths yourself, a couple of oils that you use are useful to rub onto your dog's collar. Lavender is quite good, but the best of all is rose geranium. Some of this on your dog's collar will repel ticks quite effectively. Even better – a tiny drop of rose geranium oil into your dog's bath will be enough to make those critters scuttle!

Nose Butter

- Frequently, with changing climatic conditions, dogs noses will suffer from drying and cracking. Never fear, make this great 'nose balm' in advance and be prepared! Get yourself some little tins or plastic containers before you start to make it and then realise you don't have anything to put it in!
- If you live in a really cold climate, rub this into the dog's nose before you go out. Dry he or she thoroughly on return and rub some more onto the nose. You will only have one problem – they will definitely try to lick it off!

Neem Oil

- Great for human skin and for dogs too! A natural healing oil or cream that soothes irritation and replaces the suppleness in dry skin.

Oatmeal Paste

- Talking of itching – it can drive you mad let alone poor pooch – mix some fine oatmeal with water and rub the paste into the affected area. Leave for 10 to 15 minutes and rinse off thoroughly. Really does work!

Vitamin E Oil

- ❖ Dry or itchy skin – try rubbing a little Vitamin E oil into the affected skin – this will lubricate the skin and ease the irritation. You can also use the oil in your dog's bath, but do treat one thing at a time – too many combinations of oils etc in one bath could exacerbate any one of the conditions by being too strong. Try massaging your dog with the oil – its therapeutic for both of you!

Yogurt

- ❖ A classic way to soothe your dog's tummy – mix with a little probiotic and prebiotic supplement and he will love you forever – they love the taste and it is so good for them.

Other Homemade Remedies

Nose Butter

Ingredients:

- 2oz/55g beeswax
- 2oz/55g shea butter
- 1fl.oz/30ml calendula or lavender infused olive oil
- 3 drops cardamom essential oil

Method:

Melt the beeswax, shea butter, and olive oil together. Remove from the heat, stir in the essential oil, and pour into a tin to set. Store in a cool, but not too cold place.

Dry and Cracked Paws Balm

Ingredients:

- 2fl.oz/60ml olive or sweet almond oil
- 2fl.oz/60ml coconut oil
- 1oz/30g shea butter
- 4tsp beeswax

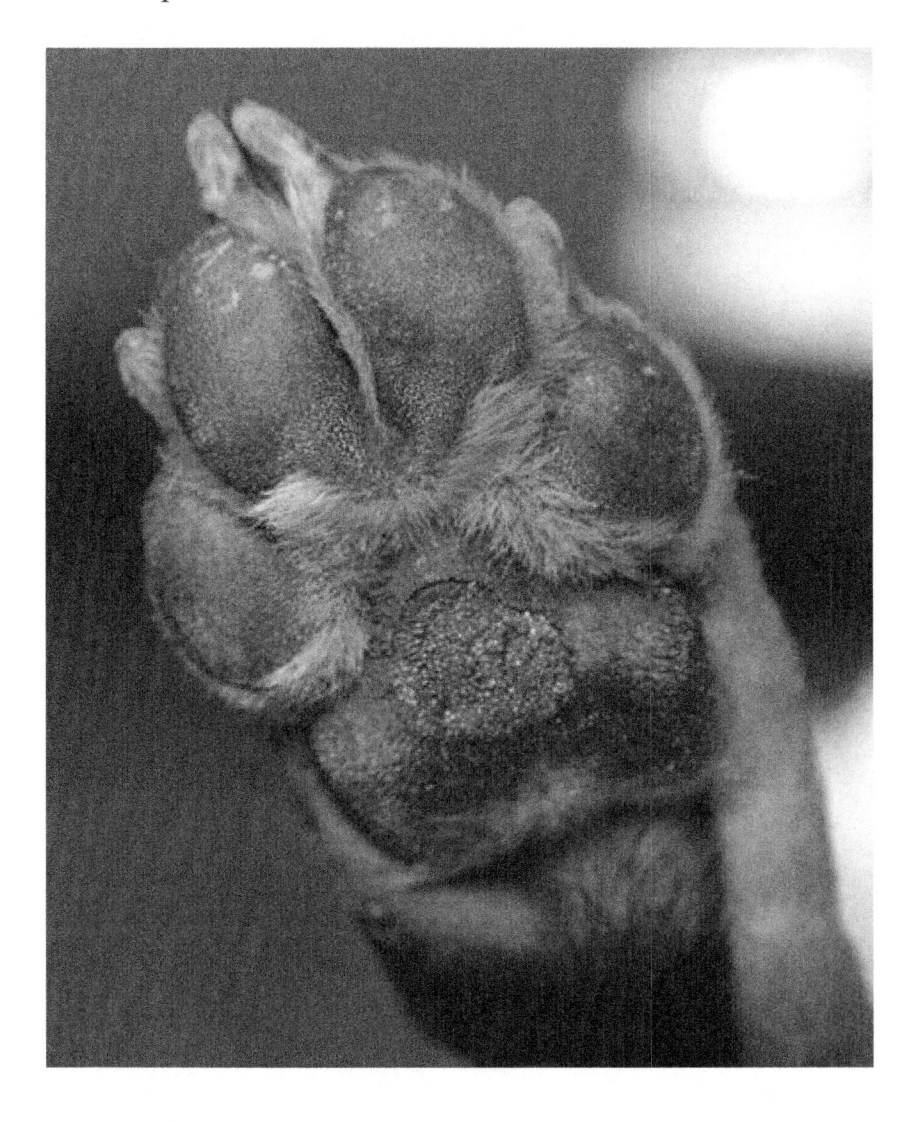

Method:

In a small pot – or double boiler – over low heat melt the oils, shea butter, and beeswax. Stir continuously until all is melted and well blended.

Pour the mixture into lip balm tubes and/or tins.

Leave to cool

Store in a cool place away from heat

You can add other restorative ingredients such as vitamin E oil, calendula oil, and other friendly skin oils such as lavender. Only a few drops so as not to make the smell overpowering.

Printed in Great Britain
by Amazon